MW00630077

*That prayer is most likely to pierce heaven
which first pierces one's own heart.*

Thomas Watson
(1620–1686)

PIERCING HEAVEN

PRAYERS
of the
PURITANS

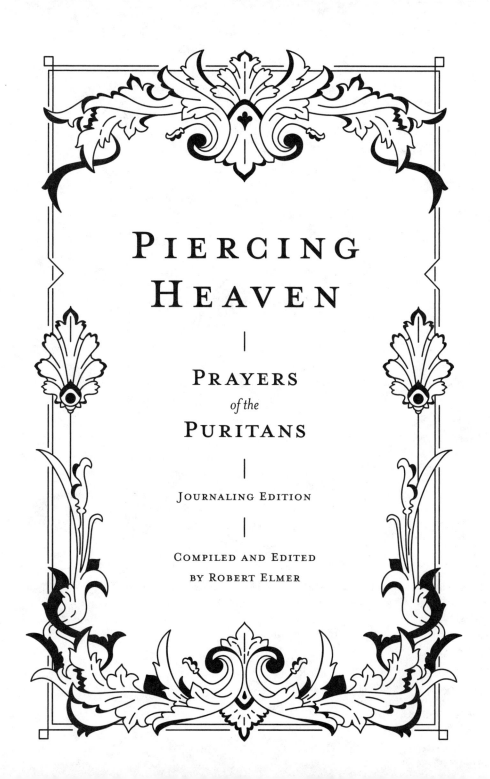

PIERCING HEAVEN

PRAYERS
of the
PURITANS

JOURNALING EDITION

COMPILED AND EDITED
BY ROBERT ELMER

Piercing Heaven: Prayers of the Puritans
Journaling Edition

Copyright 2022 Robert Elmer

"Praying and Journaling with the Puritans as Your Guide"
  copyright 2022 Jenny-Lyn de Klerk

Lexham Press, 1313 Commercial St., Bellingham, WA 98225
LexhamPress.com

Scripture quotations are adapted from the American Standard Version (ASV). Public domain.

ISBN 9781683595762

Lexham Editorial: Mark Ward, Tom Parr, Danielle Thevenaz, Kelsey Matthews, Mandi Newell
Cover Design: George Siler
Interior Design: Abigail Stocker

The Prayers

Waiting for the King of Glory · Looking for the Daystar · Trusting God in difficult times · Jesus supplies · Let the King of Glory come in · The Almighty Breaker · Because you are Jesus · Jesus my hiding place · Jesus my friend · The heavenly show · Enlarge my heart so you may dwell there · God can, God will · Mountains are level in God's strength · Jesus the all in all · For when we doubt · You have the words of eternal life · Mercy upon mercy · Our souls pant for you

INTRODUCTION

What does it take to pray like a Puritan? And why would we want to?

For more than two centuries, a bright, passionate faith spread throughout England and across the Atlantic to its colonies—a passion that spurred service and holy living for the day along with a clear view of eternity.

The Puritan movement sought to carry the Reformation forward and "purify" the Church of England throughout the 1600s and into the 1700s on both sides of the Atlantic. Its followers sought purity of Scripture-based worship, purity of doctrine, and purity of prayer.

Their aim was neither casual nor perfunctory prayer. The prayers of the Puritans shook lives to the core, pled with a sovereign God for mercy, and praised him in the brightest sunshine of grace.

"In Puritan thinking, the Christian life was a heroic venture, requiring a full quota of energy," says Wheaton College professor Leland Ryken. "For the Puritans, the God-centered life meant making the quest for spiritual and moral holiness the great business of life."[1]

But much has changed over the past several hundred years, and we speak a very different language from these saints. That in itself is enough of a barrier between their understanding of God, and ours. As written, their words and thoughts are often difficult to decipher.

So the intent of this book is to bring back some of the most passionate examples of Puritan prayer, from earnest repentance to joyful praise.

With updated language that is edited and compiled from sermons and original writings, each prayer transports us to a time when worship was central to the health of the community, and certainly not just for an hour on the weekend.

There is serious faith entwined in these prayers—faith that can still illuminate the darkness of our world, and of our times. Just as then, the life of faith stands in stark contrast to that which surrounds us.

With that in mind, we may have much more in common with our Puritan ancestors in the faith than we could have imagined. Just read what they prayed, and pray along. In so doing, we become a living answer to the prayer of one Puritan pastor, Philip Doddridge, who asked that his writings "may reach to those who are yet unborn, and teach them your name and your praise, when this author has long dwelled in the dust."[2]

And the Rev. Doddridge wasn't the only one with a long-range perspective. Another Puritan pastor, Joseph Alleine, wrote in 1671:

> *And though I might never know it while I live, yet I beg you, Lord God, let it be found at the last day, that some souls are converted by these labors. And let some be able to stand forth and say that by these they were won to you. Amen, amen. Let the one who reads this say amen.*[3]

PURITANICAL PURITANS

The Puritans have an undeserved reputation for severity. (The very name "Puritan" was originally a slur.) And indeed, they lifted God very high, so that man might appear as nothing before him.

Matthew Henry wrote,

> *You are the blessed and only ruler, the King of kings, and the Lord of lords, who only has immortality, dwelling in the light which no one can approach, whom no one has seen or can see.*

But the Puritans believed in a biblical God, one who is not just "transcendent" but "immanent"—one who is both impossibly far and incredibly near.

Robert Hawker wrote,

> *Oh Lord, send forth today abundant streams to cleanse, revive, comfort, satisfy, and strengthen all your churches. Lord, cause me to drink of the rivers of your pleasure, for you are the fountain of life.*

This combination of awe before God's holy presence and deep, passionate love for the Christ who said, "I am with you always," marks the Puritans. Far from being haunted by the fear that someone, somewhere might be happy (H. L. Mencken's taunt about them), the Puritans knew where true and lasting pleasure was to be found.

They also discovered the great open secret of prayer: the value of praying God's words back to him. Over and over throughout their prayers, the Puritans make allusion to the Bible. It suffuses their devotion, keeping it from morphing into mysticism. It also makes them accessible to today's Christians—because the Bible is something we surely share. We can learn to pray like the Puritans.

The only way the Puritans' killjoy reputation can be maintained is through ignorance of what they actually wrote. It was not just warmhearted but ardent, not just careful but truly biblical. The prayers of the Puritans are a treasure for today.

A FEW NOTES ABOUT THE TEXT

Quotations throughout have been slightly modernized, both for spelling and for vocabulary. They have also, a few times, been turned from third-person to second-person so as to form prayers of direct address. It is testimony to the Puritans' devotional depth that this was such an easy task. They wrote before God to men.

The Puritans also wrote with a notable attention to beautiful word pictures, and any modernizing is provided with the intent to reveal rather than obscure their warmhearted eloquence. "Thee" and "ye"—which in this book have been translated into contemporary English—are valuable for distinguishing singular and plural second-person pronouns in Elizabethan English, but they tend to make modern readers sense a level of formality that the Puritan writers did not intend. Puritan writing did not sound archaic or grandiloquent to its original readers.

Not every writer in the ensuing pages is, technically, a "Puritan." But the Puritan spirit was fruitful and multiplied, spreading beyond the time and place of its birth. The non-Puritan writers included here would surely be honored to share pages with bona fide Puritan luminaries.

—*Robert Elmer*

Praying and Journaling
with the Puritans as Your Guide

For centuries, believers have turned to the Puritans as guides for Christian living because they were experts. Combining their deep knowledge of Scripture and equally deep knowledge of human nature, they developed a rich understanding of what it means to be in relationship with God. And though, according to the Puritans, spiritual disciplines like praying and journaling made up a life lived with God, the practices themselves were not the point. Rather, such practices were used to craft, with God's help, a whole-self, whole-life devotion to God—that is to say, a devotion that included every part of one's being and every aspect of one's existence. This devotion was not just a means of offering oneself to God but also of receiving his love and thus being close to him as a friend.

One of the reasons the Puritans placed such a strong emphasis on this holistic devotion was because of the weaknesses they perceived in the national church of their time. Though some were ministers in the Church of England themselves, they eventually had to draw a line beyond which they were not willing to go—and on the other side of that line was the Book of Common Prayer. However, the Puritans were not against this prayerbook itself. Rather, they were against the national church's prescription for ministers to only use its prescribed forms for public prayer to the neglect of "free prayer" or "prayer in the Spirit"— that is, prayer that relies on the Spirit's help. The Puritans believed that Christians should rely on the Spirit's help because enabling such prayer is part of the Spirit's role as the Third Person of the Godhead, according to passages like Romans 8:26.

This is a perfect example of the Puritans' emphasis on holistic devotion empowered by God himself. And it is perhaps explained best by the preeminent Puritan theologian John Owen. In his *Pneumatologia*, Owen taught that the Spirit helps us in prayer by (1) showing us our own wants and how God supplies our wants in the promises of the gospel, (2) enabling us to see Christ's beauty in these promises and to place our faith in him, and (3) inspiring in us love of and delight in God and godliness over love of and delight in ourselves and our own comfort. This kind of prayer is both sensitive to our unique needs—as the Spirit helps us to analyze our current situations, have suitable feelings and use suitable words for what we are currently going through, and pray effectively for others in our lives according to our personal relationship with them—while never losing sight of the greatness of God, his word, and his glory. Thus, Owen explained that prayer is not something utterly above us or without relevance to our specific life situations but is communicating with God using all we are, exactly where we are.

Based on this theological framework, the Puritans reasoned that though it is fine to use prayers written by other people to aid your own prayers, you must do so with a full heart and mind and must never replace the Spirit's aid in prayer. This is because a good prayer is not just saying the right things or even saying them with the right attitude or in the right position or with the right tone of voice—it is communing with God himself.

Perhaps you have experienced this before. You probably know what I mean when I say that sometimes in prayer, you are led to articulate everything you have been thinking about in a way that suddenly makes sense in light of Scripture. And in that moment, you feel God's presence with you and are reminded that he hears you, loves you, and is providentially working in even the intricate details of your life, your family, and your church, so that you leave your prayer time with a sense of deep peace about your fate and that of your friends, family, and even the universe. Jesus is paying attention, and being able to pour out your heart to this Friend of all friends shapes you, changes you, and makes you a Christian.

Such prayer in the Spirit provides a great snapshot of what Puritan spirituality was all about, and this journaling edition of Puritan prayers offers the best way for us to use their prayers and helps us think Puritan-ly about devoting our own lives to God.

In fact, journaling is another spiritual discipline that we can learn about from the Puritans. In the seventeenth century, many kept notebooks (called "commonplace books") in which they jotted down random but meaningful pieces of information. Christians often used them to keep track of Bible verses, notes from sermons, explanations of doctrines, and reflections about their lives. For example, in her notebook, the Puritan author Lucy Hutchinson wrote down two personal statements of faith, important points from Calvin's *Institutes*, a list of arguments that prove God's existence, and a poem about the love of God. Such immediacy and diversity show us that on a regular, everyday basis (even in the most difficult times of her life, like after her husband's death), she was devoting her life to God—he consumed her thoughts, filled her time, and took up space in her physical possessions.

Similarly, the Puritan philanthropist Mary Rich, Countess of Warwick, kept a daily diary in which she recorded her experiences in meditation, which were inspired by what she read in the Bible and good books as well as what she observed in nature. Such meditation influenced not only her own life but also the lives of others, as it solidified her commitment to share her knowledge of the faith with her fellow Christians; exhibit patience with her invalid husband, who struggled with anger; and give generously to the poor. Her journal entries were encouraging not only in the moment when she recorded the meditations but also in later months, when she reread her diary to remember how faithful God had been in her life.

Such energetic Christian living is also seen in a theological treatise that Hutchinson wrote for her newlywed daughter, wherein she included Bible verse citations in the margins as a means of encouraging Barbara to engage with the physical book and meaning of the text herself. As you can see, Puritan spirituality was a reading, writing, thinking, praying, moving, journaling kind of spirituality that engaged the whole person in their whole life, through the amazing, the ordinary, and even the messy.

So, as you read and journal in this volume, you might, like Hutchinson, write down ideas that come to mind, or like Rich, record how these prayers inspire you to help others. Or perhaps you might look up relevant Bible verses like

Hutchinson did, or ask for the Spirit's help and closeness as you seek to draw near to him, interpret your life, disciple others, and bask in the beauty of Christ's fulfillment of gospel promises like Owen. Regardless of what you write or say or pray, may these Puritan prayers fill your soul with dreams of Jesus and heaven, leading you to the kind of devotion that relishes in giving love and receiving it, which is so satisfying that it reminds you why and how you're a Christian in the first place.

—*Jenny-Lyn de Klerk*
author and editor at Crossway
former Puritan Project Assistant, Regent College

If any surviving friends should, when I am in the dust,
come across this memorial of my transaction with you,
may they make it their own.

PHILIP DODDRIDGE
(1709–1751)

LIST OF AUTHORS

JOSEPH ALLEINE (1634–1668)

RICHARD ALLEINE (1610/11–1681)

ISAAC AMBROSE (1604–1664)

WILLIAM AMES (1576–1633)

RICHARD BAXTER (1615–1691)

LEWIS BAYLY (1575–1631)

ANNE BRADSTREET (1612–1672)

WILLIAM BRIDGE (1600–1670)

THOMAS BROOKS (1608–1680)

JOHN BUNYAN (1628–1688)

ANTHONY BURGESS (1600–1663)

JEREMIAH BURROUGHS (1599–1646)

STEPHEN CHARNOCK (1628–1680)

DAVID CLARKSON (1622–1686)

ARTHUR DENT (died 1607)

PHILIP DODDRIDGE (1709–1751)

WILLIAM GURNALL (1616–1679)

WILLIAM GUTHRIE (1620–1665)

ROBERT HAWKER (1753–1827)

MATTHEW HENRY (1662–1714)

GEORGE HERBERT (1593–1633)

EZEKIEL HOPKINS (1633–1689)

JOHN HOWE (1630–1705)

JOHN OWEN (1616–1683)

ROBERT PARKER (1564–1614)

EDWARD REYNOLDS (1599–1676)

JOHN ROBINSON (1575–1625)

RICHARD SIBBES (1577–1635)

NATHANAEL VINCENT (1639–1697)

GEORGE WHITEFIELD (1714–1770)

OCTAVIUS WINSLOW (1808–1878)

HERMAN WITSIUS (1636–1708)

THE PRAYERS

TEACH ME TO PRAY.

Our Lord's prayer

Our Father, you are seated on a throne of glory in the highest heaven, and we bow before your awful presence with humble reverence. Even so we approach you with the confidence that we are your children, and you are our bountiful and compassionate parent.

We join our prayers to you with hearts full of brotherly love, and ask for each other the blessings we seek for ourselves.

Above all, we desire your glory. May your name be set apart and holy. May the whole world of living creatures join us to give you the honor you so deserve and require. May your kingdom come and your will be done among us. Help us to know, understand, and pursue your kingdom.

And may your will, always wise and gracious, be done on earth just as it is in heaven. Teach us mortals to resign ourselves to you in obedience, the same way your angels in heaven obey you.

As for ourselves, Lord, help us not to seek the grand things of life. Help us not to worry about the future, but we humbly ask that you would open your bountiful hand—the one on which we always depend. Give us our daily supply for what we need today, and teach us to let you take care of the rest.

Though in many respects we have been disobedient and ungrateful children, yet we beg you, compassionate Father, to forgive us our offenses. We know we are guilty in your book, with debts we can never repay. But please forgive those debts, even as we forgive others—even those who have offended and injured us. We ask for the same kind of pardon we are willing to extend to others.

And do not bring us into places of pressing temptation, where we would lose our integrity and our soul would be endangered. But if we must be tried, graciously rescue us from the power of the evil one, that he would not triumph.

We know you can do these things for your children, and we humbly trust you will, because yours is the universal kingdom, the fullness of almighty power, and the glory of infinite perfection. To you be the praise of all, forever.

Amen. So may it be. We sincerely and earnestly desire that you may be glorified and our prayers heard and accepted. Amen.

— *Philip Doddridge*

PREPARE ME TO SEEK YOU

O Lord, teach me to pray, that I may call upon your name. Prepare my heart to seek, and open your ears mercifully to hear me.

Almighty and eternal Lord God, you are the Creator and Continual Preserver of all things, both in heaven and earth. By your gracious providence I was at first fearfully and wonderfully made, and even now you keep me and preserve me.

I am the workmanship of your hands, and I desire to humble both soul and body before your heavenly majesty.

So here in your presence, Lord, I confess my own unworthiness to come before you, to call upon you, or to perform the least duty that will concern your worship and glory.

Because my heart is polluted and unclean, I beg you to be gracious to me for Jesus Christ your Son's sake. For the sake of his promise, truth, and mercy, have mercy upon me.

Pardon and forgive all the sins, iniquities, and trespasses I have ever committed against you, in what I have said or what I have done. Amen.

— *Robert Parker*

Help Me Ask
for Help!

NO HOPE WITHOUT CHRIST'S RIGHTEOUSNESS

Lord, I would be the most miserable person in the world if my hopes were only in this life. Why? Because I am hopeless without Christ's righteousness. My life could never be comfortable, and there would be no hope at all of eternal life.

If you denied me that hope, I would be the most miserable one of all. I may be happy without worldly enjoyments, but all things in the world cannot make me happy without this.

So however you treat me in this world, whatever you deny me, Lord, deny me not this. I can be happy without riches and abundance, like Job and Lazarus were. I can be happy even if I am reviled and reproached, as was Christ and his disciples. I can be happy and comfortable in prison, as were Paul and Silas.

But I cannot be happy without the righteousness of Christ.

All the riches, places, or honors on earth will leave me miserable if I am without this. Even if I were rich and needed nothing, without this I would still be wretched and miserable, poor, blind, and naked.

If I had all things that a person could desire on earth, what good would it do me without Christ's righteousness?

What would riches do for me, if they came with the wrath of God? What comfort would honor bring me, if I remained a son of perdition or a child of wrath?

What sweetness would there be in pleasure, if I were on the path to everlasting torments?

What miserable comforts and enjoyments are these, without Christ's righteousness!

Lord, however you deal with me in outward things, whatever you take from me, whatever you deny me—do not deny me Christ! Do not deny me a share in his righteousness! Amen.

— *David Clarkson*

THE COMMANDER AND HEARER
OF PRAYER

You who commands and hears prayer! You who helps your people to pray!

Pour out the spirit of grace and supplication, that your throne of grace may be surrounded by supplicants, that there may be a great flocking to the mercy seat, and grace may be imparted abundantly to your own glory, through Jesus Christ the high priest, who is passed into the heavens, and is at your right hand forever. Amen.

— *Nathanael Vincent*

A CRY FOR RENEWING GRACE

We cry to you, God, for renewing grace. We lie at your footstool and cry, "Help, Lord, or I will perish!"

Create in me a new heart, and renew a right spirit within me.

Renew me in the spirit of my mind, and renew me in my inner soul.

Take away this old mind that is so blind, so vain, so carnal.

Take away this old will that is so obstinate, so perverse, so rebellious.

Take away this old conscience that is so partial, so seared, so senseless.

Take away this old heart that will never delight in, comply with, or submit to you.

Let old things pass away, let all things become new. You who brought this world out of nothing with a word, can with a word work in me this new creation.

Do not let me perish. Say the word, and it will be done. Just say the word, and this soul—now a dark, woeful chaos and a lump of corruption and confusion—will become a new creature.

Lord, give me this new heart, put this new spirit into me. You have the key of David. You close, and no one opens. You open, and no one can shut. Lord, open this heart that has been too long closed against you. Break down these strongholds that keep you from me.

Cast out sin and cast out the world that kept you out of possession for so long. Bind the strong man and cast him out.

Other lords have had dominion over me; they have made me miserable by keeping my Lord, my happiness, from me. Cast out these intruders, take possession of me, and be mine forever.

You call for my heart, Lord; it is yours. Though I have dealt treacherously with you, and given my heart to other things, it is yours. It cost you dearly. So enter, take possession of it.

You knock at the door to this wretched heart. Why stay so long outside? Come in and bless me with your presence. Break it open with almighty power, and let it no longer shut you out. Amen.

— *David Clarkson*

I THIRST FOR GRACE IN CHRIST

Merciful Lord God, you are Alpha and Omega, the beginning and the end. You say "It is done" of things that are yet to come, so faithful and true are your promises.

You have promised by your own word, out of your own mouth, that to anyone who is thirsty you will give the fountain of the water of life freely.

O Lord, I thirst. I long for one drop of mercy. As the deer pants for the water, so my soul pants for you, O God, and for your compassion.

If I had the glory, the wealth, and the pleasure of the whole world—if I had ten thousand lives, joyfully I would lay them down, just to have this poor trembling soul received into the bleeding arms of my blessed Redeemer.

O Lord, my spirit within me is melted into tears of blood. My heart is splintered in pieces. Out of the place of dragons and of the shadow of death, I lift up my thoughts, heavy and sad, before you.

The memory of my former vanities and sins is poison to my soul. The very flames of hell, Lord, the fury of your just wrath, the scorchings of my own conscience, have so wasted and parched my heart that my thirst cannot be quenched.

My desire is for the pardon and grace of Jesus Christ. And Lord, in your blessed book you cry, "Every one who thirsts, come to the waters." In that great day of the feast, you stood and cried, "If any man thirsts, let him come to me and drink."

And these are your own words: "Blessed are those who hunger and thirst after righteousness: for they shall be filled."

I challenge you, Lord, in my extreme thirst for you, and for spiritual life in you, by that word, and by that promise which you made—make it good to me. I grovel in the dust and tremble at your feet.

Open now that promised well of life. For I must drink or else I die. Amen.

— *Isaac Ambrose*

Give me Jesus

Lord, you have given me a portion in the world. You have given me credit and a reputation among others.

But what is all this to me, if I am without Christ? If I do not have the one who gives grace to my soul, the one who is my all in all?

Lord, you have taught me this day that the distance between you and me is so great that without a mediator, I perish forever.

So whatever else you deny me, give me Jesus. Amen.

— *Jeremiah Burroughs*

RENEW ME IN GRACE

O Lord, I have no graces by nature. I have no power to cleanse my own heart.

I have defaced your image, but I cannot repair it. I can say with the apostle that when I want to do well, evil is present with me, but I find no means to do what I desire.

Oh when will I be set free to do the work of God, and run the race of his commands? If only I had hope, joy, and love!

Lord, I have heard of your power. You call things that are not, as if they were. If you desire it, you can work in me these graces, just as you gloriously created them in Adam.

Lord, I have also heard of your grace and truth. You are as faithful to keep as you are generous to make these precious promises. Your grace is unsearchable. Your word is purer than silver, seven times refined. Oh make good your promises! Replenish me with your grace! Amen.

— *Isaac Ambrose*

IS MY NAME WRITTEN ON GOD'S HEART?

Lord, I have not done my duty in my own family, among
Christians, in the churches of Christ. I have not done what
I promised. I have not served my generation or helped to
build the building of Zion.

And now, Lord, what can I say?

Is my name written on the heart of Christ? If I had the
whole world's glory, if I had ten thousand worlds, and ten
thousand lives, I would lay them all down, to have my
poor trembling soul assured of this.

My thirst cannot be quenched, and my desire for Jesus is
as greedy as the grave, with coals of fire and the hottest
flame.

Lord, you have said you will wed me forever, so this is
what I desire. Fulfill what you have spoken! It would break
my heart if ever the covenant should be broken between
me and you. I desire you, Lord; and the more I enjoy
you, the more I desire you with an infinite, eternal, and
everlasting desire. Amen.

— *Isaac Ambrose*

CREATE IN ME A NEW HEART

Create in me, O Christ, a new heart, and renew in me a right spirit. Then you will see how I will serve you as your new creature, in a new life, after a new way, with a new tongue and new manners, with new words and new works, to the glory of your name, and the winning of other sinful souls to your faith.

Keep me forever, O my Savior, from the torments of hell and tyranny of the devil. And when I am to depart this life, send your angels to carry me, as they did the soul of Lazarus, into your kingdom. Receive me into that joyful paradise you promised to the penitent thief, who at his last gasp upon the cross begged for your mercy and admission into your kingdom.

Grant this, O Christ, for your own name's sake. I give you all glory, honor, praise, and dominion, both now and forever. Amen.

— *Lewis Bayly*

COMING TO THE HIGH PRIEST

Lord Jesus, our great high priest, surely you are faithful. Surely you will do the work of the high priest for my soul.

I have sinned, and sinned greatly. But Lord, it is the work of our high priest to clear my debt. Now, Lord Jesus, I come to you as my high priest. Resolve this for me.

I confess that my own conscience accuses me. Satan accuses me. Moses accuses me. But it is the work of our great high priest to remove all accusations brought against poor believers.

So now Lord, I do come to you as my great high priest. Take away the accusations. When I look at what I do, there is so much deadness, so much hardness of heart, and so many distractions. I am afraid my best will never be enough.

But Lord, it is the job of our great high priest to take away the weeds of the work we do, and to present it to God. Now, O Lord, I come to you as my high priest. Carry my prayers to God the Father.

When I consider my former life, Lord, I can only conclude that I am a poor sinner, and cursed. Yet it is the job of our great high priest to bless the people.

So Lord, I come to you now as my high priest. Bless me! And by your grace, tell me to increase and multiply. Amen.

— *William Bridge*

GRACE FOR THE WEARY

Lord, we know your words, "The Lord God has given me the tongue of those who are taught, that I may know how to sustain with words the one who is weary."

I am one of those wearied souls, Lord. I am wearied with my temptations, wearied with inward trouble.

So now, Lord, speak a word in due season to this poor, wounded, and wearied soul.

Let me serve you, Lord—that is all my desire. Let me see you as you please, when you please.

I am done, Lord, I am done. I have questioned and questioned my condition these many years. And I see there is no end of such questioning. I get nothing by it.

I am a poor, weak creature, and I fear I will never be able to bear testimony of the truth of Jesus Christ. But you have said, "I will give to my two witnesses." I am one of your witnesses. Now then, Lord, give power to me, for I am poor.

I see the sinfulness of sin, so let me also see the graciousness of grace, and the fullness of Christ. I come to you for righteousness, because I see my sin is exceedingly sinful.

O Lord, keep my soul in the ocean of your free love. Amen.

— *William Bridge*

I WILL WAIT FOR YOU TO LEAD ME

Lord, I am hungry for righteousness—but I cannot find
it. And I hope this will be my concern forever: whatever
becomes of me, I will reject unrighteousness. I pray that I
will not meddle with it and will have nothing to do with it.
Through your mercy I hope to keep that prayer forever in
my heart.

Lord, if there be but one drop of mercy in me to show pity
to others, is there not an infinite ocean of mercy in you?

And Lord, you who know the secrets of all hearts, you
know the desire of my soul to know your will.

Whatever help you make known to me, I am ready to
make use of it, that I may not be led aside into error. And
if you are pleased to reveal your mind further to me, I am
ready to submit to it. I would count it greater happiness
than all the comforts the world can afford simply to know
your mind.

But, Lord, as yet I cannot do this thing without sinning
against you. You know it. Yet you also know that I want to
walk humbly and peaceably with others, in all meekness,
submissiveness, and quietness of spirit.

I will wait until you further reveal your mind to me. Your
light will turn my spirit the way you want it to go.

— *Jeremiah Burroughs*

Awake my sleeping heart

O injured, neglected, provoked Benefactor: when I think
but for a moment of all your greatness and goodness, I
am astonished at the indifference in my heart. I blush and
cannot lift up my face before you.

I have played the fool and made a significant blunder.
And yet this foolish heart of mine would make its having
neglected you so long a reason to keep neglecting you.

Every one of your rational creatures should be all duty and
love for you. Each heart should be full of a sense of your
presence. A desire to please you should swallow up every
other desire.

Yet you have not been in all my thoughts. And faith,
the end and glory of my nature, has been so strangely
overlooked.

I know, if matters rest here, I perish. Yet I feel in my perverse
nature a secret reluctance to pursue these thoughts. I am
prone to lay them aside for now, or even to dismiss them
entirely.

My mind is perplexed and divided. But I am sure that you
who made me knows what is best for me.

So I ask that you will, for your name's sake, lead me and
guide me. Do not let me delay until it is forever too late.

Pluck me as a brand out of the burning. Break this fatal
enchantment. Let me finally come to the place where I am

not tempted to wish you never made me, or that you could forever forget me. The place where I fail to recognize my best hope, and perish.

O God, let me hear and obey you! Let your grace teach me the lesson I am so slow to learn, and let it conquer the strong opposition in my heart. Hear these broken cries, for the sake of your Son. He has taught many others who are just as stubborn as I, and he "is able from these stones to raise up children for Abraham." Amen.

— *Philip Doddridge*

PRAYER FOR A NEW HEART

Lord, is it not better to make me your friend than to let me continue as your enemy?

Would you not be glorified more by raising a soul from sin than a Lazarus from the grave? Your power and mercy are shown greater by turning a dry stump into a fruitful and flourishing tree. So overcome my shameful nature by your merciful power. Change me from a venomous to a dove-like nature.

I would be made happy to glorify you by becoming what I was created to be! Glorify yourself by creating my heart anew, that I may glorify you in newness of life.

I cannot get a new heart by my own strength, but it is not too hard for your power, and it matches your promise. Amen.

— *Stephen Charnock*

Show me the way from your word, 1

Blessed God, I humbly adore you as the great Father of lights, and the Giver of every good and every perfect gift (James 1:17).

I seek every blessing from you, and especially those which may lead me to yourself, and prepare me for the eternal enjoyment of you.

I adore you as the God who searches the hearts and tries the reins of the children of men (Jeremiah 17:10).

Search me, O God, and know my heart; try me, and know my thoughts. See if there be any wicked way in me, and lead me in the way everlasting (Psalm 139:23–24).

May I be renewed in the spirit of my mind (Ephesians 4:24).

You give me a new heart, and place a new spirit within me (Ezekiel 36:26).

Make me a partaker of the divine nature (2 Peter 1:4), and as he who has called me is holy, may I be holy in all I say (1 Peter 1:15).

May the same mind be in me which was also in Christ Jesus (Philippians 2:5), and may I walk even as he walked (1 John 2:6).

Deliver me from being carnally-minded, which is death; and make me spiritually-minded, since that is life and peace (Romans 8:6).

And may I, while I pass through this world, walk by faith and not by sight (2 Corinthians 5:7) and be strong in faith, giving glory to God (Romans 4:20).

May your grace teach me to deny ungodliness and worldly lusts, and to live soberly, righteously, and godly (Titus 2:11–12).

Work in my heart the kind of godliness which is profitable for all things (1 Timothy 4:8).

Teach me by the influence of your blessed Spirit, to love you with all my heart, soul, mind, and strength (Mark 12:30).

May I yield myself to you, as alive from the dead (Romans 6:13) and present my body as a living sacrifice, holy and acceptable in your sight, which is my most reasonable service (Romans 12:1)! Amen.

— *Philip Doddridge*

SHOW ME THE WAY FROM YOUR WORD, 2

Father, may I have the most faithful and affectionate regard to the blessed Jesus, your incarnate Son, the brightness of your glory, and your exact image (Hebrews 1:3).

Though I have not seen him, may I love him; and in him, though now I do not see him, yet believing, may I rejoice with unspeakable joy, full of glory (1 Peter 1:8).

May I live daily by faith in the Son of God (Galatians 2:20).

May I be filled with the Spirit (Ephesians 5:18) and led by the Spirit (Romans 8:14), and so may it be evident to others that I am a child of God, and an heir of glory.

May I not receive the spirit of bondage to fear, but the Spirit of adoption, crying, "Abba, Father" (Romans 8:15).

Work in me a spirit of love, power, and of a sound mind (2 Timothy 1:17), so that I may add virtue to my faith (2 Peter 1:5).

May I be strong and courageous (Joshua 1:7) and act like a Christian in the work to which I am called.

May I labor, not only or chiefly for the food that perishes, but for that which endures to eternal life (John 6:27).

May I humble myself under your mighty hand and be clothed with humility (1 Peter 5:5–6), with a meek

and quiet spirit, which is valuable in the sight of God
(1 Peter 3:4).

May I be pure in heart, that I may see God (Matthew
5:8); put to death whatever belongs to my earthly nature
(Colossians 3:5).

May I be content with such things as I have (Hebrews
13:5) and learn to be that way in all circumstances
(Philippians 4:11).

May patience also have its full effect in me, that I may be
complete and lacking nothing (James 1:4).

May I love my neighbor as myself (Galatians 5:14), and do
unto others as I would want them to do unto me (Matthew
7:12). Amen.

— *Philip Doddridge*

A PRAYER FOR OUR CHILDREN

Lord, may you answer our united prayers with peace.
Pour out your Spirit on our families, and your blessing on
our children, that they may grow up before you as willow
trees by the river, that they may be a comfort to their
parents, a support to the church, and a name and a praise
to you. Amen.

— *Philip Doddridge*

Show me the way from your word, 3

Lord, may I put on meekness under the greatest injuries and provocations (Colossians 3:12), and, as much as it depends on me, may I live peacefully with all (Romans 12:18).

May I be merciful, as my Father in heaven is merciful (Luke 6:36).

May I speak the truth from my heart (Psalm 15:2) and may I speak it in love (Ephesians 4:15), taking care not to judge severely, as I would not want to be judged.

Work in me the kind of disposition you approve. Renew a right spirit within me (Psalm 51:10) and make me a genuine son of Israel (John 1:47).

And while I feast on Christ, as my passover sacrificed for me, may I keep the feast with the unleavened bread of sincerity and truth (1 Corinthians 5:7–8).

Make me steadfast and immovable, always abounding in your work, knowing that my labor in the Lord will not be in vain (1 Corinthians 15:58).

Keep my heart tender (2 Kings 22:19), easily impressed with your word and providence, touched with an affectionate concern for your glory, and sensitive to every impulse of your Spirit.

May I be zealous for you, God (Numbers 25:13), with a zeal based on knowledge and love (1 Corinthians 14:14). Teach me in your service to join the wisdom of the serpent with the boldness of the lion and the innocence of the dove (Matthew 10:16).

In this way make me, by your grace, a shining image of my dear Redeemer. May I ascribe everlasting honors to him; and to you, O Father of mercies; and to your Holy Spirit, through whose gracious influence I may call you my Father; and Jesus my Savior! Amen.

— *Philip Doddridge*

TO THE GARDENER OF MY SOUL

Oh, precious Jesus—may I be no longer unfruitful in your garden!

Lord, do as you have said. Dig around me, and pour on me all the sweet influences of your Holy Spirit—which, like the rain, the sun, and the dew of heaven, may cause me to bring forth fruit to God.

And, Lord, if you will listen to an unworthy creature like me plead for others, let the coming year bring the same blessings to all your redeemed—even to my unawakened relatives, and to thousands who are still in darkness.

I pray that this may be to them the acceptable year of the Lord! Amen.

— *Robert Hawker*

Breathing in grace

Ever-blessed fountain of natural and spiritual life! I thank you that I live, and that I may live a faith-filled life.

I bless you that you breathe into me your own living breath.

Though I was once dead in my sins, now I have become a living soul, in a sense that is unique to your own children.

But I do not just want to live. I want to grow in grace, and in the knowledge of my Lord and Savior Jesus Christ (2 Peter 3:18).

So I beg you to form my mind in the image of faith. Do not let me misunderstand grace, measuring my growth in grace by a natural yardstick.

Let me experience your love even more, with unreserved resignation to your wise and holy will, and a greater care for others.

Strengthen my soul as you help me grow in patience, in humility and zeal, and in a heavenly attitude. Give me a concern to be accepted by you (2 Corinthians 5:9).

Whether I live or die, let everything I do be for your glory.

You know I hunger and thirst after righteousness. Make me whatever you want me to be.

Draw your image on my soul. By the gentle influences of your Spirit, trace every feature which your eye, O Heavenly Father, may enjoy, and which you may see as your own image.

I know I am not yet where I should be. I am far from being already perfect. But after the great example of the apostle, I forget what lies behind, and strain forward to what lies ahead (Philippians 3:13).

Feed my soul by your word and by your Spirit. Then I will be born again, not of corruptible seed, but incorruptible— even by your word, which lives and abides forever (1 Peter 1:23). As a newborn babe, I desire the sincere milk of the word, that by it I may grow (1 Peter 2:2).

And may my progress be obvious to all (1 Timothy 4:15) until I finally reach maturity, to the measure of the stature of the fullness of Christ (Ephesians 4:13).

And after having enjoyed the pleasure of those that flourish in your courts below, I will come to live in the paradise above!

I ask and hope this through our Lord and Savior Jesus Christ—to whom be glory, both now and forever. Amen.

— *Philip Doddridge*

GRACE TO LIGHT OUR LIVES

Light up, O Lord, a brighter and a stronger flame in the lamps of your sanctuary.

Send the arrows of your quiver deep into our conscience. Clothe your priests with salvation, that your saints may shout aloud for joy! Anoint them with your Holy Spirit, that the aroma of your grace may spread throughout all your tabernacles, like fragrant oil poured on the head of Aaron.

Lead us, O Lord, in the way everlasting. Make us resemble our great Master, more and more, as we show grace to others.

Sanctify our hearts by your grace, that we may be as trees bearing good fruit, or like fountains of pure streams. That is the path to lay up good treasure—it is the way for holiness and compassion to spring forth in freedom, to refresh and give life to everyone around us.

May your grace animate our souls, Lord. May nothing stand in the way of faithfulness even to death, or deprive us of the crown of life your grace has promised.

Send forth laborers into your harvest, and energize them in their work. Give us a deeper sense of that horrible condemnation due to those who despise their divine Master and his Heavenly Father, in whose name he was sent.

Preserve us from that kind of guilt and ruin, God! Your kingdom has come to us, and its privileges. May we never abuse them and be cast down to hell, but may divine grace open our hearts to the gospel.

May we receive all those who faithfully proclaim your word, and welcome them in the name of Jesus. Amen.

— *Philip Doddridge*

Melt our hearts

Visit each of our children and young friends, O Lord, with your mercy. Animate them to walk in your truth and bless them—even when nothing remains of all the love we have bestowed but the memory of our exhortations and examples.

Fill and expand our hearts more and more with true generosity. May we act toward strangers, and especially fellow believers, in a way that is worthy of you, whenever they need our assistance. And especially let our love abound to those who have a desire to spread the gospel.

Send forth, O Lord, the gentle influences of your Spirit. Melt those hearts which will not be broken by the weightiest strokes of your vengeance, and deliver us from the tempter. Amen.

— *Philip Doddridge*

GIVE US A NOBLER MIND

Have pity, O Lord, upon our weakness, and give us a better mind to understand the true sense of your word.

Give us a simplicity of heart to receive it, the integrity to declare it, and a zeal to teach and defend it.

And while we are doing so, or while we are doing any other work you have assigned us, wherever you place us in life, whatever difficulties may surround us, whatever sorrows may depress us, let us with pleasure hear you proclaiming, "Behold, I come quickly; and my reward is with me, to give to each man according to his work."

Let us hear you say that you are coming to receive your faithful persevering people to yourself, to dwell forever in that blissful world, where knowledge, holiness, and joy will be poured in upon our souls in a more immediate, nobler, and more effectual manner.

Amen, even so come Lord Jesus!

Hasten the blessed hour to us, and to all your churches. And in the meantime, may your grace be with us to keep alive the remembrance of your love, and the expectation of your coming, in our hearts.

Animate us to be and act in a way that honors the blessings we have already received, and the nobler joy you have taught us to seek. Amen and amen.

— *Philip Doddridge*

HOW THEY LOVE EACH OTHER

Gracious Emmanuel, send down your spirit of love on all your followers, that we may no longer glory in the little distinctions of any faction or denomination.

Instead, may we show we are Christians, standing together under your glorious banner!

May we wear your mark of honor on our shoulders, or like a crown on our heads.

In that way may the spirit of hatred, disgrace, and persecution vanish like a noxious mist before the sun.

And may it again be said everywhere, as it once was:

"Look how those Christians love each other!"

Amen.

— *Philip Doddridge*

FIGHTING THE GOOD FIGHT

Grant, dearest Lord, that though we still live in this world, yet never, never may we forget our relationship to you. Though we are outcasts, yet we are Jesus' outcasts.

Lord, be our hiding place, so that you are all we need, like "streams of water in a dry place; like the shade of a great rock in a weary land."

Oh for a word, a whisper of Jesus. I cannot live without it. I dare not let you go, unless you bless us. None of all the past enjoyments or experiences will do us any good, until you again shine in upon my soul. Come then, Lord Jesus! I fly to you as my God, my Savior, my portion, my all!

I see my daily, hourly, continual need of you. You are our hope and Savior! Keep me, Lord, near you, for without you I am nothing.

Precious Jesus, help me to see my clear part in you, from my union with you. And dear Lord, make me so strong in your strength, that during the whole period of my present warfare, I may be "awesome as an army with banners" to all who would oppose my way to you, and in you.

Yes, Lord! Let sin, and Satan, and the world, be united against me; yet put on me the whole armor of God, that I may "fight the good fight of the faith, take hold of eternal life," and be made "more than conquerors through the one who loved us" Amen!

— *Robert Hawker*

SEEKING JESUS FOR YET MORE GRACE

Jesus, Master, have mercy upon me! I wake this morning poor, wretched, empty, and needy—as though I never before had heard of your dear name, or had never been living upon your fullness.

But you know I cannot live upon the alms of yesterday, no more than my body can stay healthy from the food I ate many days in the past. Without a new supply, Lord, I know that I am yours, and that you are mine.

So I come to you for a new supply, and surely you will not send me away empty.

Lord, I rejoice even that I feel my poverty—that way, as an empty vessel, I am better suited to receive your fullness.

Give in, blessed Jesus, to my poor hungry soul. Then I will find a reason to rejoice that my emptiness and begging pushed me to seek you, and that my need gave you an opportunity to display your grace.

Yes, blessed Lord, I am not only content to be poor and to be needy, but to be nothing, to be worse than nothing. As long as you receive glory by showing your love and giving out of your riches, I will glory even in my infirmities, that the power of Christ may rest upon me.

A beggar still I wish to be, and to lay at your gate, if only to glimpse your face, and to receive one token from your fair hand. Then am I most full, when most empty, to be filled with Jesus. Amen.

— *Robert Hawker*

Preparing for battle

Dearest Lord Jesus! Day by day, and in the evening and night, let your sweet visits renew us without ceasing.

Then I will take this precious portion my song, both when undressing for the bed of sleep, and for the bed of death: "In peace I will both lie down and sleep; for you, Lord, alone make me dwell in safety."

May I never lose sight of Gethsemane. Let me return here by faith, and see you "exceedingly sorrowful, even to death," that your sacred head might be lifted up, first on the cross in suffering, and then with your crown in glory!

Lord, keep me from every enemy who does evil in your sanctuary, and preserve all those tender graces of your Spirit, that I may bring forth fruit to the praise of your holy name, and may flourish and spread abroad as the cedar in Lebanon.

Dearest Jesus, I know this in theory, from your gracious teachings, and I know that I am by nature a sinner. But I always fail, when I come to put it into practice.

Teach me, Lord, how to keep it always in mind, that I may never go forth in holy warfare to subdue a single foe except in your strength, and never mention anything but your righteousness, only your righteousness.

Blessed Sun of Righteousness, shine with such warm, life-giving, fruit-imparting beams of your rich grace upon my soul, that I may flourish under your divine influence, and show that "the Lord is upright; he is my rock, and there is no unrighteousness in him." Amen.

— *Robert Hawker*

COME, HOLY SPIRIT

Come, Holy Spirit, with all your sweet and precious favor. Come, Lord, to convince and comfort me, to humble and direct me, to chill my affections to the world, and to warm them toward the Lord Jesus.

Come, you holy, gracious, almighty reviver and restorer— and glorifier of my God and Savior!

Cause the graces you have planted in my soul to go forth in a way of love and desire, faith and expectation. Let me hope in the person and glory of the one my soul loves. Then I will cry out with the church, "Let my beloved come into his garden and eat his precious fruits." Amen!

— *Robert Hawker*

No one speaks like Jesus

Precious Lord Jesus, how will I express my soul's sense of your love and grace, your mercy and favor?

Since you first revealed yourself to my heart, I am no longer my own. You have taken all my affections with you to heaven, and caused them to center everything in yourself.

So now, Lord, every day—sometimes every hour—when I hear your voice, I have to cry out, "No one ever spoke like this man!" (John 7:46).

Your words are sweet and perfect for my weary soul, and my sense of nothingness makes your fullness even more precious.

When I hear you say "My grace is sufficient for you, for my power is made perfect in weakness" (2 Corinthians 12:9), I feel a power that makes all my enemies seem as nothing.

Like your servant, I then truly "glory in my weaknesses, in order that the power of Christ may rest on me."

Be all I need, dearest Lord. Let me hear your voice and see your countenance. Because both in life and in death, in time and to all eternity, the voice of my Lord Jesus will be my everlasting comfort.

No one speaks like you! Amen.

— *Robert Hawker*

HELP US TO PRAY

Many may ask, "Who will help us?"

We say, "Lord, show us your face." That will give us glad hearts, even so much more than farmers after a great harvest.

We ask your favor and acceptance with our whole heart. Hear our prayer, Lord, and in your faithfulness answer us. Be close to us in everything. You that hear the young ravens cry, do not be silent. Otherwise we are like those who go down to the pit.

Let our prayer be to you like incense, and may our outstretched hands be acceptable in your sight.

We beg for the powerful help and influence of the blessed Spirit of grace in our prayers. We do not know what to pray for as we ought. But let your Spirit help our illnesses, and pray for us.

Pour upon us the Spirit of grace and prayer. Through the Spirit of adoption, teach us to cry, "Abba, Father!" Send your light and truth; let them lead and guide us to your holy hill and your tabernacles. Lead us to you, God, our exceeding joy.

Lord, open our lips, and our mouth will praise you. Amen.

— *Matthew Henry*

I NEED THE COMFORTER

Blessed promise! Holy Spirit, make it happen in and upon my soul, day by day.

Bring me under the continued baptisms of your sovereign influence, and cause me to feel all the sweet anointings of the Spirit sent down upon the hearts and minds of your redeemed. These are the fruits and effects of Jesus, the promise of God the Father.

Yes, blessed Spirit, cause me to know you in your person, work, and power.

I need you day by day as my Comforter.

I need you as the Spirit of truth, to guide me into all truth.

I need you as the one who reminds me of the Lord Jesus, to bring to my forgetful heart all the blessed things he has revealed to me.

I need you, as the witness of my Jesus, to testify of my wants, and of his fullness to supply.

I need you as my advocate and helper, in all my infirmities in prayer.

I need you as the deposit of the promised inheritance, that I may not faint or lack faith to hold on and hold out in every dark season.

I need you, Lord. I cannot do a moment without you, nor act in faith, nor believe a promise, nor exercise a grace, without your constant hand on my poor soul.

Come then, Lord, I beg you, and let me be brought under your unceasing baptisms. Shed abroad the love of God my Father in my heart, and direct me into the patient waiting for Jesus Christ. Amen.

— Robert Hawker

TEACH ME GRACE

Lord, you have made a covenant of grace with a poor person. This covenant of grace is founded on the priestly office of Jesus Christ.

The new covenant promises that we will all be taught by God. Lord, I am ignorant! Teach me by the work of Christ, that I may be made wise in salvation.

Lord, you have made a covenant of grace with a poor man, a covenant which says, "I will put my law within them."

So now, Lord, seeing that Jesus Christ has founded this covenant in his blood, and I am one of those for whom he made satisfaction: write your law in my inward parts, that I may do all your will. Amen.

— William Bridge

BE PLEASED WITH US, IN HIM

Lord, you have said that you will be set apart in those who approach you, and before all people you will be glorified. So we worship you, Lord, to glorify your name.

We call on you to deliver us. For all things are of you, and through you, and to you.

We do not approach you in prayer because of our own righteousness. Our sins prevent us from standing before you, but we make mention of Christ's righteousness—his alone. He is our righteousness.

We know that spiritual sacrifices are acceptable to you only through Christ Jesus. And we cannot hope to receive anything, unless we ask you on his behalf.

Therefore make us accepted in the Beloved, the one who adds much incense to the prayers of saints, and offers them up upon the golden altar before the throne. We come in the name of the great high priest, who is passed into the heavens, Jesus the Son of God.

He was touched with the feeling of our infirmities, and is therefore able to save to the uttermost all those that come to God by him. He lives forever, making intercession.

See our shield, O God, and look on the face of your Anointed. With a voice from heaven, you declared yourself well pleased in him. Lord, in him be well pleased with us. Amen.

— *Matthew Henry*

MY REASON EMPLOYED FOR YOUR TRUTH

Lord, here is a heart that I strive to make and keep void of offense. Please fill it with your promised grace and Spirit.

Of course my heart is not a mansion pure enough for the pure and holy God. Even so, will you accept it and dwell here? There are still many hidden corruptions, but search them out. And you, who have kept your servant from obvious sins, would you also cleanse me from secret faults?

Lord, I am blind and ignorant, and I cannot see through to the consequences. Things that I think are for my advantage may prove to be a snare and a curse.

But in your infinite wisdom you know everything, so I resign my choice to you. Choose for me. And however your providence will order my affairs, make me then as thankful for disappointment as I ought to be for success.

Lord, your word has taught me many mysteries which my weak and short-sighted reason cannot comprehend. But I desire to sit at your feet; your word will shape my outlook. And this I understand: you who are very truth can neither deceive nor be deceived. So I find infinitely more reason to believe anything you tell me than to disbelieve it—even if it seems impossible.

Since you have spoken it, I fully assent. And I deliver up all the cheeky impudence of my reason to be chastised and tutored by faith. Amen.

— *Ezekiel Hopkins*

Prayers from George Whitefield's Journal

Oh when will I be free from indwelling sin? Lord deliver me from this body of death!

Deal with me as it pleases you, Lord. You may justly take everything from me, for I have abused your lovingkindness. God be merciful to me, a sinner.

What am I, that I should be fed daily with heavenly manna? Lord, you fill my soul. Let me praise you with joyful lips.

I adore your infinite goodness that reaches down to me. Do not leave me to myself, but purge me for your mercy's sake, that I may bring forth more fruit. Correct me when I go astray, and lead me in your perfect way.

Dearest Lord, for your mercy's sake never let me distrust you again! Oh me of little faith.

Lord, your judgments are like the great deep. Your footsteps are not known. Just and holy are you, O King of saints!

In the season of night, let me arise and give you thanks. Let my speech be of your lovingkindness and tender mercies, all day long.

May it be my sleep, my food and drink, to do the will of my Heavenly Father.

You who holds the wind in your fists, and the waters in the palms of your hands, accept our thanks for your past mercies. Set apart our travels, and if it is best, carry us with speed to where we should go. Send me wherever and whenever it seems good to your divine majesty.

Raise my heart and make your power known in the hearts of your people. Add daily to your church those who will be saved. They are noted in your book; let them also be written on my heart.

And now let your servants depart in peace, for our eyes have seen and our hearts have felt your salvation.

Even so come Lord Jesus, come quickly. Amen and amen.

— *George Whitefield*

ASKING, RECEIVING

Did you not say, Lord, "If you ask anything from the Father, he will give it you in my name. Up till now you have asked nothing in my name; ask, and you shall receive, that your joy may be made full" (John 16:23–24)?

I am encouraged by this saying. So I come now for large supplies of your grace, mercy, pardon, and peace. I seek you, Jesus—you yourself, with your gifts, with all your fullness, and all your blessings.

And I am sure, if you will give me as large a hand to receive as my Lord's hand is to give, I will be blessed. Amen.

— *Robert Hawker*

HELP ME THROUGH
MY DOUBTS.

A PRAYER FROM ONE STILL ON THE FENCE

Righteous and holy Sovereign of heaven and earth:

My breath is in your hand. All my ways are in your hand. But I confess I have been far from glorifying you, or conducting myself according to your will.

So I have reason to adore your forbearance and goodness, that you have not long since stopped my breath, and cut me off from the land of the living.

I appreciate your patience. Thank you that I did not, months and years ago, become an inhabitant of hell, where ten thousand delaying sinners are now lamenting their folly, and will be lamenting it forever.

But God, it is very possible that this trifling heart of mine may ultimately betray me into the same ruin.

I am convinced that, sooner or later, I must give serious thought to faith, or I am undone. And yet my foolish heart draws back from the yoke. I stretch out on my lazy bed, and call for a little more sleep.

My corrupt heart pleads against the conviction of my better judgment. Lord, save me from myself! Save me from the deceit of sin! Save me from the treachery of my perverse nature, and fix upon my mind what I have been reading!

I have heard the warnings about the uncertainty of life and the day of salvation. I have made a few lightweight goals, and have begun to take tiny steps in your direction.

But I have only been fluttering around faith. All my intentions have been scattered like smoke, or a vapor before the wind.

Bring these things home to my heart, now, with a more powerful conviction than ever. Pursue me with them!

And if I should be insane enough to try to escape again, let your Spirit use the language of terror. Employ your most powerful tools to awaken me from this deadly stupor— even if it interrupts my workday, or my sleep.

From this moment, Lord, may I be able to recognize a more lasting impression of faith than anything yet made on my heart. Amen.

— *Philip Doddridge*

INCREASE MY FAITH

Jesus, Master, look upon me, put the earnest cry in my heart, that I may unceasingly, with the apostles' prayer, send forth this as the first and greatest petition of my whole soul: *Lord, increase my faith.* Amen!

— *Robert Hawker*

VENTURE ALL FOR CHRIST

O Lord, I am a fool, and not able to know the truth
from error. Leave me not to my own blindness, either
to approve of or condemn this doctrine. If it be of God,
let me not despise it. If it be of the devil, let me not
embrace it.

Lord, I lay my soul in this matter only at your feet. Let me
not be deceived, I humbly beseech you.

Lord, Satan tells me that neither your mercy nor Christ's
blood is sufficient to save my soul. Lord, will I honor
you most, by believing you will and you can? Or him, by
believing you neither will nor can?

Lord, I will gladly honor you by believing you will and
can.

I am for going on, and venturing my eternal state with
Christ—whether I have comfort here or not. If you do not
come in I will leap off the ladder, even blindfolded, into
eternity. Sink or swim, come heaven, or come hell—Lord
Jesus, if you will catch me, do.

If not, I will venture for your name. Amen.

—John Bunyan

GIVE ME A HEART TO BELIEVE

Lord, for too long I have been disobedient to the heavenly call and resisted your holy will.

But now I want to follow your will, as far as I know it.

I have no way to know it but by the word, and that speaks plainly. It is your command I should believe.

Let your will be done in my heart, Lord. Let this law of faith be written in my inward parts.

If it were not your will, I would dare not ask, and I could not expect it. But since it is your will, Lord, let it be done on earth, as it is in heaven.

What may be done, if the will of God may not be done? What may I seek, if not your will?

And what does a person gain, unless it helps fulfill your will? If I should ask of you riches, or long life, or great things for myself, it would be my will rather than yours.

But it is your will that I should believe. Lord, not my will, but yours be done.

Give me a heart to believe, that I may obey you, for you have commanded it. Give me a heart to believe, that I may please you, for you have said that is what you desire. Give me a heart to believe, that I may honor you, for you have declared that this gives glory to you.

Lord, let me be your servant, even the lowest of servants, just so I may have a place in the family. Whatever my condition or capacity, I will be thankful not to be disowned.

It is enough to be yours. Just give me a heart to believe, since without faith I can have no part in you.

Lord, you have let some light into my mind and conscience. Do not let it end in darkness. Let it be like that light which shines more and more into a perfect day.

The spirit of conviction has awakened my soul. Do not let it end in a spirit of slumber. Do not let your sparks be extinguished.

All your works are perfect. Carry this work to perfection. Amen.

— *David Clarkson*

GIVE ME FAITH!

Give me faith, Lord, or I die! I may live without friends, wealth, honors, or pleasures, but I cannot live without faith. There is nothing but death for me in unbelief.

Lord, whatever you deny me, do not deny me faith. I am lost, undone, I perish, I am a dead man without faith. It would have been better if I had never been born, than to live in unbelief.

Your wrath would weigh on me while I lived in this horrible state, and it would be that way forever.

I will never see life, unless I believe. There is no hope for me until then. My case is miserable and desperate until I believe, and I can never believe unless you give me faith.

Lord, give me faith, or else I die.

It is miserable to be excluded from life—to be dead while I live! Unless you give me faith, I will never see life.

What misery it is to be under divine wrath! How unavoidable the misery of those who are under abiding wrath!

What joy can I have in any enjoyment, when your wrath is mixed with all? What comfort can my life be to me, if your wrath hangs continually over me?

Lord, hear me! Bring my soul out of this mire and clay, out of unbelief, out of the pit where there is no water, no comfort, no refreshment, and no relief.

You take no pleasure in the misery of wretched creatures. It is no delight to you that I am miserable, but rather that I should live.

Lord, give me faith, or else I will never see life. Give me faith, or else I will be forever miserable.

— *David Clarkson*

FROM ONE DEGREE OF FAITH TO THE NEXT

Blessed God, I acknowledge before you my own weakness and insufficiency for anything that is spiritually good.

I have experienced it a thousand times, and yet my foolish heart would again trust itself and resolve to move ahead in its own weakness.

But let this be the firstfruits of your gracious influence: to bring it to a humble distrust of itself, and to rest in you.

I rejoice, O Lord, in your assurance that you are ready to shower me with rich benefits. So because of your kind invitation, I boldly approach your throne, to find grace for help in every time of need.

I do not mean to turn your grace into a license for immorality or to make my weakness an excuse for negligence and laziness. You have already given me more strength than I have used.

I want to be found diligent in the use of everything you supply. If not, any petition like this one would be a profane mockery, and would probably provoke you to take away what I have, not impart more.

But as I firmly resolve to exert myself, I ask for your grace to fulfill that resolution.

Fill me with the right attitude toward you and my fellow creatures. Remind me always of your presence, and that every secret of my soul is open to you.

May I guard against the first sign of sin, and may Satan find no room for his evil suggestions. Fill my heart with your Holy Spirit, and take up your residence there.

Dwell in me, walk with me, and let my body be the temple of the Holy Spirit.

Take me from one degree of faith, love, zeal, and holiness, to the next, until I appear perfect before you through Jesus Christ my Lord. In him I have righteousness and strength. Amen.

— *Philip Doddridge*

HELP ME THROUGH
MY TIME OF SADNESS
AND SUFFERING.

WHEN I AM SICK

You have refreshed my soul, Lord, with many sweet songs, when all the world was to me asleep, and could not interrupt my happiness.

How often have I been blessed with the harmony of the songs of redemption, and run over in some of the blessed verses of it.

Jesus has loved me, and given himself for me. Yes, Lord! I think I have been often awakened in the night by you, and I have found my soul instantly led out by your grace, to a sense of your presence, and to a desire for you.

Precious Redeemer, grant me frequent visits, and sweet messages of your grace. And if in your wise and kind providence, sickness, or pain, or afflictions are at any time appointed me, stay by me, Lord. Keep my heart in sweet recollection of you. That way, in the multitude of my heart's sorrows, your comforts may refresh my soul.

— *Robert Hawker*

PRAYER FOR A DYING FATHER

I turn to you in my doubt and uncertainty, Lord. I know that you live forever. You are the one who determines life and death. You bring us down to the grave, and only you can say, "Return!"

So if there is still room for prayer, please hear mine on your servant's behalf: Would you spare him yet a while, that he might recover strength once more?

But if he is out of reach of this prayer, help us to accept your wise will.

We adore your name, and your praise mingles with our tears. And though we mourn the loss of our loved one, even so we rejoice to think that we do not mourn like those who have no hope.

Because to live is Christ, and to die is gain. Amen.

— *Philip Doddridge*

In time of suffering

Gracious Lord!

Nothing can reconcile us to you better than to humbly and patiently learn obedience in the school of suffering.

We learn by knowing that Jesus, though you are the Son of God, in the eternity of your nature you were pleased in your human nature to learn obedience by the things which you suffered.

Precious Jesus! To your love, and your grace, be all praise and glory. Under your banner of love alone we are more than conquerors.

Come then, blessed Lord, in all your fullness. I desire only you. With my soul have I desired you in the night. And now, with the first dawn of day, I seek you early.

Surely, when you come, as I know you will come, you will in deed and in truth be the tree of life. My soul is now opened by you to meet you. So Lord, show me your person, glory, grace, and love, and fill every portion of my heart.

As I wait for your coming, I pray that my view of your grace and sense of my unworthiness may melt my whole soul before you and your presence.

And how refreshing it is to know that, "Since the children are sharers in flesh and blood, you also yourself likewise took part of the same things."

So when my poor heart is afflicted, when Satan storms, or the world frowns, when I suffer sickness, or when all your waves and storms seem to go over me, what relief it is to know that you, Jesus, see me. And that you care!

So help me, Lord, to look to you, and remember you. And oh! That blessed Scripture: "In all their affliction he was afflicted, and the angel of his presence saved them. In his love and in his pity he redeemed them; he bore them and carried them all the days of old." Amen.

— *Robert Hawker*

IS MERCY GONE?

Lord, you know I have been carried along many times toward what is good, carried against my own nature. You know I have been carried further in a good way than I ever intended.

You know when my soul has been dead and hardened. I have said, mercy is gone—and then you have persuaded me that Jesus Christ is in me. Amen.

— *William Bridge*

NO SORROW LIKE YOURS

There was no sorrow like your sorrow, Lord—no love like your love. Was it not enough, dearest Savior, that you came down to pray, and sigh, and weep for us? Would you also bleed and die for us?

Was it not enough that you were hated, slandered, blasphemed, buffeted? But you would also be scourged, nailed, wounded, and crucified.

Was it not enough to feel the cruelty of man? Would you also experience the wrath of God?

And if your love was not enough, giving up your life and shedding that precious blood, was it not enough to die once, to suffer one death? Would you die twice by tasting the first, and something of the second death—suffering the pains of death in both soul and body?

Oh the far-surpassing love of Christ! Heaven and earth are astonished at it. What tongue can express it? What heart can conceive it? The tongues and the thoughts of people and angels are far below it.

Oh the height, and depth, and breadth, and length, of the love of Christ! All creation knows not how to react. Our thoughts are swallowed up.

And there they remain until glory elevates them, when our job will be to praise, admire, and adore this love of Christ. Amen.

— David Clarkson

HELP ME ENDURE
TEMPTATION.

A PRAYER FOR DELIVERANCE FROM THE WORLD

Blessed God! In the midst of ten thousand snares and dangers, let me look to you with the humble prayer that you would deliver me from those who rise up against me (Psalm 59:1) and that your eyes are on me for good (Jeremiah 24:6).

When laziness is about to seize me, awaken me from idle dreams with a lively view of that invisible and eternal world to which I am headed!

Remind me how important it is to make the most of the moments you give me—time to prepare for eternity.

When sinners entice me, may I not consent (Proverbs 1:10). May my conversation with you give me a distaste for the conversations of those who are strangers to you— those who want to separate my soul from you.

May I honor those who fear the Lord (Psalm 15:4). And by spending time with wise and holy people, may I advance daily in wisdom and holiness (Proverbs 13:20).

Bring me to life, O Lord, so that by me you may also enliven others!

Make me the happy instrument to kindle and animate the flame of divine love in others. May the flame catch and grow from heart to heart!

Guard me, Lord, from a love of sensual, earthly pleasure. May I remember that to set my mind on the flesh is death (Romans 8:6).

Purify and refine my soul by your Holy Spirit. Help me to reject unlawful pleasures more than others pursue them, but to carefully and moderately use the ones you allow.

May my soul rise on the wings of holy thoughts to a place of invisible glory.

Powered by your grace, let me learn to entertain angels that live in your presence. They are happy not to be brought down by the worst earthly distractions, which often cause us to forget our original higher purpose.

Help me to know my God-given place, and to keep at the work you have given me. But deliver me from the burdensome cares of this world, which would so absorb my time and thoughts that "the one needful thing" would be forgotten.

Moderate my desires for worldly possessions by reminding me how uncertain and unsatisfying they are. So while others are laying up treasures on earth, may I be rich toward God (Luke 12:21).

May I never be too busy for those great things which lie between you and my soul.

May I never be so engrossed with the concerns of time to neglect the interests of eternity!

May I pass through earth with my heart and hopes set
upon heaven, and feel the attraction stronger and stronger
as I approach nearer and nearer to that center we seek—
until the happy moment comes when every earthly object
disappears from view, and the shining glories of the
heavenly world fill my improved and strengthened sight.

Then I will be cheered by that which would now
overwhelm me. Amen.

— *Philip Doddridge*

A PRAYER FOR REVIVAL

Eternal, unchangeable Lord! Your perfections and glories
will never change. Jesus your Son is "the same yesterday
and today and forever" (Hebrews 13:8).

The closer the eternal world gets, the more I must consider
it. But sadly, my views, my affections, and my best
intentions keep changing—just like my poor body.

Where do these changes come from, Lord? And what
about the way my soul feels alienated from you?

Why can I not just come to you with the affection of a
child, as I once did? Why do I avoid serving you? It was
once my greatest pleasure. Now it seems like a burden.

Where is the blessing I once had? My joy in you as my
Heavenly Father was so obvious that strangers could not
miss it. My heart overflowed with so much love to you,

and passion for serving you, that it felt like self-denial not to express it.

Where did I fall? You see me still, but I am not the same. I blush to see how cold and indifferent I have become.

When you see me in secret, you see me amusing myself with trivial things, when I used to spend my time serving you.

You see me coming into your presence as if I was forced. And when I am before you, my spirit is so empty that I hardly know what to say to you—though you are my God, and there could never be anything more important than time spent with you.

Even when I do speak with you, my prayer is cold and formal. What happened to the passion I once felt, the intense pursuit of you, O God?

And what happened to the wonderful rest I had in you, that feeling of just being happy to be near you—and my determination to never stray from your presence?

I am so far removed from that place. When my short devotions are over—if you can even call them devotions—I forget about you for the longest time.

I am so barely animated by your love, or interested in serving you, that a stranger might talk with me for a long while and not have a clue that I knew you, or had even ever heard of you!

You call me to your house, Lord, on your own day. But my worship is heartless.

I present you with nothing more than my body. My thoughts and affections are engrossed in other things. I draw near you with my mouth, and honor you with my lips—but my heart is far from you (Isaiah 29:13).

You call me to your table, but my heart is so frozen, it hardly melts even at the foot of the cross. It hardly feels any power in the blood of Jesus.

I am such a wretched creature, unworthy of being called yours! Unworthy of a place among your children, even the lowest place in your family.

I am worthy to be cast out, forsaken, even utterly destroyed.

Is this the dedication I once promised you, and which you have so many reasons to expect?

Is this my response to your daily care? For the sacrifice of your Son, the presence of your Spirit, the pardon of my numberless sins? For the undeserved and so often forfeited hopes of eternal glory?

Lord, I am ashamed to stand or kneel before you. But pity me, I beg you, and help me. My soul lays itself in the dust before you. Give me life, according to your word (Psalm 119:25)!

Do not let me waste any more time—I am at the edge of a cliff!

Give me grace to turn toward your testimonies, without further delay, that I may keep your commandments (Psalm 119:59–60).

Search me, Lord, and try me. Get to the root of this disease which spreads itself over my soul, and heal me.

Show me my sin, Lord, that I may see its horror. Show me Jesus in such a light that I may look upon him and mourn, that I may look upon him and love (Zechariah 12:10).

May I awaken from this lethargy into which I am sinking, and may Christ give me a more abundant spiritual life than ever. Alive in him, let me recover the ground I have lost—and then gain yet more!

Send your Spirit on me to dwell in a temple consecrated to himself (1 Corinthians 3:16), and may he direct my holy and acceptable sacrifice of service (Romans 12:1).

May the incense be constant and fragrant! May the sacred fire burn and blaze perpetually (Leviticus 6:13)! And may none of its vessels ever be profaned by unholy or forbidden use. Amen.

— *Philip Doddridge*

SEARCH ME, LORD

Come, blessed Spirit, Author of all grace and consolation. Show me my sin in all its worst colors, that I may feel an unwavering hatred of it.

Show me the majesty and mercy of God in such a way that my heart will be alarmed and melted. Convince me, O you blessed Spirit, of sin, righteousness, and repentance.

Show me that I have undone myself, but that my help is found in God alone, in God through Christ, in whom alone he will extend compassion and help to me.

Show me the power of Christ to save! I teach my faith to see him extended on the cross, arms open wide, with a pierced, bleeding side, telling me what room is in his heart for me.

May I know what it is to have my whole heart subdued by love, so subdued as to be crucified with Christ, to be dead to sin and dead to the world, but alive to God through Jesus Christ.

May I confide in his power and love. May I commit my spirit to him without reserve. May I bear his image, observe his laws, and pursue his service.

And through time and eternity may I remain a monument of the power of the gospel, and a trophy of his victorious grace.

O blessed God, if there is any secret sin yet lurking in my soul, anything I have not sincerely renounced, show me and tear it out of my heart—even if it has shot its roots ever so deep, and wrapped them all around, so every nerve would be pained by the separation. Tear it away, Lord, by your graciously severe hand.

By degree, by speed, perfect what is still lacking in my faith. Accomplish in me all the good pleasure of your goodness.

Enrich me, Heavenly Father, with all the grace of your Spirit. Form me into the complete image of your dear Son. And then, for his sake, come to me and manifest your gracious presence in my soul, until it is ripened for glory. Amen.

— *Philip Doddridge*

CALL MY WANDERING HEART HOME

Dear Lord of your people, let every evening toll the bell of recollection to call home my poor wandering heart.

And when the tumult of a busy, unsatisfying, and troublesome world is over, oh for grace to do as my Lord did: to send the multitude away, and get up apart into the holy mountain of faith and love in the Lord Jesus, to meditate and pray! Amen.

— *Robert Hawker*

I AM HUNTED WITH TEMPTATION

Lord, I am hunted with temptation. Either you must pardon it, or I am condemned. Kill it, or I will be a slave to it.

Take me into the bosom of your love for Christ's sake. Castle me in the arms of your everlasting strength.

It is in your power to save me from, or give me up into the hands of my enemy.

I have no confidence in myself or any other. Into your hands I commit my cause and myself. I rely on you.

I will be your true prisoner. I would rather die by the hand of your justice than continue fighting against your mercy.

Lord, here I am, willing to deliver up all I have and am, to be at your disposal. My will will be done when you put your will in me.

Cut and carve me however you please, that at last I may be polished and framed according to the plan which love has drawn into your heart for me.

All my gifts and services do not please you, unless with them I give you myself. In the same way, none of these gifts of your bounty can make me content, unless you bestow yourself on me with them. Amen.

— *William Gurnall*

LET ME NOT SIN AGAINST YOU

Lord, keep me from yielding to sin, whatever I suffer. How could I do such wickedness? How could I neglect this duty and sin against you, God?

For your sake, Lord, let me not sin against you. You are good. You are kind. You are gracious. You are holy.

Will I sin or rebel? For your sake, Lord, I will not do it. I will not for my own sake. In sinning against God, I sin against my own soul. Sin and death, sin and hell are linked together.

Even if it were not so, Lord, I will not sin against you. You are good in yourself and good to me. You are my God and my Father.

Love, care, tenderness, compassion, and kindness are all in your heart toward me.

What I am, what I have, what I hope for, that I breathe, that I live—all is your goodness and your bounty to me.

Do not let me rise up against the one that bore me and fed me. I would never return evil for good—not to my child, my fellow laborer, or my friend. And let me never do so to you, my Father and my God!

Do not let this evil which I fear ever come upon me. Put your fear into my heart, Lord, that I may not sin against you. Amen.

— *Richard Alleine*

I NEED YOUR PROTECTION

Blessed God! I flee to your almighty power.

You see me surrounded with difficulties and dangers, and stretch out your omnipotent arm to save me.

Today I put myself under your protection. Let me make the shadow of your wings my refuge. Let your grace be sufficient for me, and your strength be made perfect in my weakness.

I dare not say, "I will never forsake you, I will never deny you," but I hope can truly say, "Lord, I resolve not to do it. I would rather die than offend you."

Root out the corruption from my heart. In an hour of pressing temptation it might sway me to view things in a different light, and so might betray me into the hands of the enemy!

Strengthen my faith, Lord, and encourage my hope! Inspire me to opposing every thing that blocks my way to heaven. And let me set my face against all the assaults of earth and hell.

If sinners entice me, let me say no. If they insult me, let me ignore it. If they threaten me, let me not fear!

Give me instead a holy and ardent yet prudent and well-governed zeal to see others convicted and turn to you.

Let me never be ashamed to plead your cause against those who oppose the faith. As the psalmist says, "Make me to hear joy and gladness ... then I will teach transgressors your ways, and sinners will be converted to you."

My fears continue, Lord, but there is no one to blame but myself. I join you in blaming me for my folly.

Keep me, O Lord, now and always. Whatever age or place in life I attain, never let me think I am strong enough to maintain the combat without you.

And even in my young faith, never let me imagine myself so weak that you cannot support me.

Wherever you lead me, let me follow. Wherever you take me in life, let me work there faithfully. Let me fight the holy war against the enemies of my salvation. And let me fall fighting rather than abandon my post.

You are my glorious Redeemer, pioneer of my salvation, the great Author and Finisher of my faith. When I am in danger of denying you, as Peter did, look on me with your majesty and tenderness. Keep me from falling, or quickly lift me back up to God and my duty again!

Show me how to learn from my missteps and to humble myself in even greater diligence and caution. Amen.

— *Philip Doddridge*

I WRESTLE WITH SIN

You are my Lord and God, and I will serve you.

I have chosen you as my inheritance forever, and I will wait for your salvation.

Hear the sighing of your prisoner, and deliver your captive. My heart is with you.

I pray that sin would no longer reign in my mortal body. I want nothing more to do with the throne of iniquity. Untie the chains, loosen the cuffs, and bring my soul out of prison.

Search me, Lord, and know my heart. Prove me, and know my thoughts. Is there any way of wickedness in me? Do I willingly go after sin's commandments? Do I harbor iniquity in my heart?

It is true: My heart wars against you. It riots and rebels against you.

But do I resign myself to it? Is it a pleasure to me? Am I at peace with it?

Lord, you know. I cannot rid myself of the iniquity in my heart, I cannot do the things that I would, I cannot pray as I would. I cannot listen as I would—nor think, nor speak, nor live as I would.

Wherever I go, sin goes with me. Where I stay, it stays. If I sit still, there it is with me. If I run from it, it follows me.

I cannot rest, I cannot work, I cannot do anything—sin is always hounding me.

And yet, blessed be your name, this I do: I fight against it. I wrestle with it, though it so often takes me down. I do not trust it, though it flatters me. I do not love it, though it feeds me.

My heart is with you, Lord. I am following after you. I groan and I struggle in pain, waiting for your redemption. Until I die, I will not give up.

I will die fighting. I will die hoping. I will die praying.

Save me, Lord. Do not delay, my God. Amen.

— *Richard Alleine*

STRENGTH TO STAND UNDER TEMPTATION

O Lord, I have no strength to stand against this great enemy. I confess it is my duty to resist this temptation, but it is your promise to support me under this temptation. Therefore I put myself upon you. Amen.

— *William Bridge*

HELP ME REST IN
GOD'S LOVE.

GOD STOOPS TO THE WEAK AND UNWORTHY

Who are we, and what is our father's house, that you have brought us here?

And now, O Lord God, what will your servants say to you? We are silenced with wonder, and must sit down in astonishment. We cannot utter the least of your praises.

What does the height of this strange love mean? And what does it mean to us, that the Lord of heaven and earth should condescend to enter into covenant with dust, and take into his bosom the viperous brood that has so often spit their venom in his face?

We are not worthy to be as the handmaids, to wash the feet of the servants of our Lord; how much less are we worthy to be your sons and heirs, and to be made partakers of all these blessed liberties and privileges you have settled upon us!

But for your goodness' sake, and according to your own heart, you have done all these great things. Even so, Father, because it seemed good in your sight.

This is why you are great, O God, for there is none like you, nor is there any God besides you. Amen.

— *Joseph Alleine*

GOD HAS MARRIED HIS PEOPLE

What nation on earth is like your people?

You, God, came to redeem us as a people for yourself.
You have confirmed us to yourself, to be a people for you
forever; and you, Lord, have become our God. Wonder, O
heavens, and be moved, O earth, at this great thing!

The tabernacle of God is with us, and you will dwell with
us, and we will be your people; and you yourself will be
with us, and be our God.

We are astonished and ravished with wonder, for the
infinite breach is made up, the offender is received, God
and man reconciled, and a covenant of peace entered into.
Heaven and earth are all agreed upon the terms.

O happy conclusion! Will the stars dwell with the dust?
Or the wide distant poles be brought together?

But here the distance of the terms is infinitely greater.
Rejoice, O angels; shout, O seraphim; O all you friends of
the bridegroom, be ready with the marriage song.

Look, here is the wonder of wonders: for you, Lord, have
betrothed yourself forever to your hopeless captives, and
you declare the marriage before all the world. You have
become one with us and we with you.

You have bequeathed to us the precious things of heaven
above, and the precious things of the earth beneath, and
you have kept back nothing from us.

And now, O Lord, you are that God, and your words are true. You have promised this goodness to your servants, and have left us nothing to ask from your hands except what you have freely granted already.

Establish forever the word which you have spoken concerning your servants. Do as you have said; and let your name be magnified forever, saying, "The Lord of armies, he is the God of Israel."

Amen, hallelujah!

— *Joseph Alleine*

IN THE BEAUTY OF JESUS

In your beauty, blessed Lord, we see a fullness of grace, truth, and righteousness. It corresponds exactly to the wants of poor sinners—your blood, to cleanse. Your grace, to comfort. Your fullness, to supply.

In you there is everything we can want: life, light, joy, pardon, mercy, peace, happiness here, glory hereafter.

Do I not see you, my King, in your beauty, when I behold you coming with all these for me? So I must cry out with the psalmist, "I love you, O Lord, my strength. The Lord is my strength and song; And he has become my salvation."

And that is not all. Because when I see the King in his beauty, I see him also in his love. Yes, blessed Lord, you are so beautiful, for you have so loved poor sinners that you give yourself for them.

And we know that our love for you did not come first, but your love to us came first. Your love prompted ours. Your love filled our hearts and, by your Spirit, first prompted our minds to look toward you. That makes you lovely indeed.

And now, Lord, every day's view of you increases that love, and brings home your beauty more and more. The more often you stoop to visit my poor soul, the more beautiful you appear.

Every appearance, every view, every glimpse of Jesus, tends to make my God and King more gracious and lovely to my soul, and adds fresh fervor to my love.

Come then, you blessed, holy, lovely one, and ravish my spiritual senses with your beauty, that my whole soul would be filled only with the love of Jesus every day. Until that day when, from seeing you here below, through your grace, I come to look upon you, and live forever in your presence, in the full beams of your glory in your throne above.

— *Robert Hawker*

THE SHEPHERD OF NEW BELIEVERS

Great Shepherd of your sheep, is this how you deal so
sweetly with your little ones? That explains why young
believers, in the first seasons of knowing you, find so
much blessed refreshment.

You gather the lambs and carry them in your bosom.
You do this in a way that fully proves your love and
compassion for the needs of your flock.

Yes, Lord, you are the one who restores my soul. Praises to
your name, for you do it all in such a way that proves it to
be for your great name's sake. Your grace comes freely and
without reprimand.

"He restores my soul; he guides me in the paths of
righteousness for his name's sake."

Dear Lord Jesus! Grant me this happy frame of mind, that
I may say with David, "My heart is steadfast, O God, my
heart is steadfast I will sing and give praise!" Amen!

— *Robert Hawker*

TO THE GOD WHO BENDS DOWN TO REACH US

Precious Lord Jesus! Oh for grace to love you, who have
so loved us! You stoop to call such poor sinful people your
own, and love them as your own, and consider every thing
done for them and done to them as to yourself.

Show my poor heart a portion of that love, that I may love you as my own and only Savior, and learn to love you to the end, as you have loved me and given yourself for me, an offering and a sacrifice to God.

Precious Lord, continue to surprise my soul with the tokens of your love. All the tendencies of your grace, all the evidences of your favor, your visits, your love-tokens, your pardons, your renewings, your morning call, your mid-day feedings, your noon, your evening, your midnight grace.

All, all are among your wonderful ways of salvation, and all testify to my soul that your name, as well as your work, is, and must be, wonderful.

Jesus, you put forth your hand and touched a leper! Deal with me the same way, precious Lord. Though I am polluted and unclean, yet reach down to put forth your hand and touch me also.

Put forth your blessed Spirit. Come, Lord, and dwell in me, abide in me, and rule and reign over me. Be my God, my Jesus, my Holy One, and make me yours forever.

Yes, dearest Jesus, I hear you say that you will be for me, and not for another. So will I be for you. Oh! You condescending, loving God, make me yours, "that if I live I may live to the Lord; or if I die I may die to the Lord—so that living or dying, I may be yours."

— *Robert Hawker*

Sing the song of glory

Great, glorious, everlasting Redeemer! You are indeed both the high priest and the altar, both the sacrifice and the sacrificer. Your one offering has both put out the fire of divine wrath and caused the holy flame of love and peace to burn there instead, which has kindled in every heart of your people.

Lamb of God, you have delivered us from the wrath to come! You have made our peace in the blood of your cross.

By your blood you have quenched the just fire of divine indignation against sin. You have quenched no less than all the fiery darts of Satan. You have subdued the flaming antagonism of our hearts, with all their fiery lusts and burning affections.

What will I say to you? What will I say of you? What will I proclaim concerning you, the Lord our righteousness?

Lord, help me to begin the song, and never entertain sin or Satan—not even death itself, or allow it for a moment to interrupt the heavenly note.

Instead let your name fill my entire soul and vibrate on my dying lips, so that I may open my eyes in eternity, while the words still hang there.

"Unto the one who loves us, and freed us from our sins by his blood—unto the one who made us to be a kingdom, to be priests to his God and Father; to him be the glory and the dominion for ever and ever. Amen."

— *Robert Hawker*

ENJOYING THE FAVOR OF GOD

Lord Jesus, I seek you and your favor beyond all the riches of the earth, and all the enjoyments of the world.

Lord, help me never to forget that it was your favor that brought you down from heaven. Your favor that prompted you to die, to rise again, for poor sinners. Your favor which makes you wash us from all our sins in your blood.

All of your grace here, all the glories of redemption hereafter—everything was bought and the result of your favor.

Precious Lord, please show me your renewed favor, day by day. And let those visits from you be so gracious, so sweet, and so continual, that I may think or speak of nothing else.

I pray for grace to spend all the moments of my life here, receiving your grace and love, and bringing you love and praise, until you take me home to live at the fountain of your favor. That is when the whole happiness of eternity will be in the praises of God and of the Lamb, and we will enjoy "the favor of the one who dwelt in the burning bush."

— *Robert Hawker*

The Father planned it all

Almighty Father, it is your special mercy to give your Son, and with him all things, to the highly favored objects of your everlasting love.

From all eternity, you planned, ordered, willed, appointed, and prepared the great salvation of the gospel. You chose Christ as the head, and the church as the body of this amazing work of redemption.

You have carried out all the great designs. You strengthen and complete everything in our final salvation—in grace here, and glory hereafter.

Blessed, holy, and compassionate Lord God! For the sake of Jesus fulfill this promise daily in my soul. Bear me up, carry me through, and strengthen me in Christ, that I may walk in his name, until you bring me in to see his face in your eternal home, and I dwell under the light of his countenance forever, amen.

— *Robert Hawker*

Jesus only

Lord, when you asked Mary in her sorrow, "Woman, why are you weeping? Whom do you seek?" our souls reply with her, "We seek Jesus alone."

Oh then, to hear our own names called upon, as hers was: "Mary!" Our answer brings out every affection of the heart: "Rabbi! My Lord and my God!"

Yes! You, altogether lovely Lord, the fairest and first among ten thousand—I will go with you. I would forget my own people and my father's house. For my father's house is a house of bondage, because I was born in sin, and formed in iniquity. I am a child of wrath, just like everyone else, and by nature dead in trespasses and sins.

It is you, blessed Jesus, who have delivered me from the wrath to come. It is you who have quickened me by your Holy Spirit to a new and spiritual life. It is you who have sent your servants to call me to yourself, and have betrothed me to yourself forever.

Is there anyone who would still ask me, "Will you follow this man?"

My whole soul would outrun the question, and, like the apostle, I would answer, "To whom else will I go?"

Even the angels will witness for me. I have none in heaven or earth but you. Yes, you, dearest Redeemer! I will go with you, follow you, live with you, hang on you, die with you. Not even death itself will separate you and me.

Oh let me feel in my soul those precious words of yours, concerning your church: "I will call them my people." And my whole soul will respond to the gracious sound, and say, "The Lord is my God." Amen.

— *Robert Hawker*

THE BLESSED WORK OF THE SPIRIT

Oh blessed Spirit, to whom I owe such unspeakable mercies, let me, Lord, contemplate you today as the gracious, kind, compassionate Comforter.

For you are the Holy Spirit, the Comforter. And with mercy you sympathize with all the followers of Jesus in our afflictions, both of soul and body.

How tenderly you show us our sins, and lead us to the blood of Jesus to wash them away.

How sweetly you visit, encourage, strengthen, instruct, lead, and guide us into all truth.

And how powerfully at times, by your restraining grace, you enable us to put to death the deeds of the body, that we may live.

Holy, blessed, almighty Comforter! Continue your visits to us. Come, Lord, and abide with me, and be with me forever. Prove that you are the Sent of the Father, and of the Son, by coming to me in the name of Jesus, by teaching me all the precious things concerning Jesus, and by acting as the one who reminds us of Jesus.

In you and by your blessed work, I may know and live in the sweet enjoyment of fellowship with the Father, and with his Son Jesus Christ, through the influence of the Holy Ghost, the Comforter. Amen.

— *Robert Hawker*

I Believe—Help
My Unbelief!

TAKING HOLD OF GOD'S PROMISES

O my God and my Father, I accept you with all humble thankfulness, and I am bold to take hold of you.

O my King and my God, I subject my soul and all its powers to you.

O my glory, in you I will boast all day long.

O my rock, on you I will build all my confidence and my hopes.

O staff of my life and strength of my heart, the life of my joys and the joy of my life, I will sit and sing under your shadow and glory in your holy name.

Mine is the kingdom, the glory, and the victory. The whole Trinity is mine, all the persons in the Godhead. And look, here is the evidence—the writings which guarantee it forever.

O my God, I lay my hand on my mouth; I confess the charge of my unworthiness. My guilt and shame are such that I cannot cover them, but you can and do.

You have thrown a cloak over my nakedness, and have promised that my transgressions will not be mentioned, and that you will multiply pardons.

And will I dig up what you have buried, and frighten myself with the ghosts that infidelity has raised? Is it presumption to take the pardon that you offer, or to receive and claim you as mine when it is only what you have promised?

I would not have dared to claim any title or privilege, without your permission. I would think it was devilish pride to claim any part of you, or kinship to you, unless you showed me the way.

O my God, I see you have been at work with my soul. I find the prints; I see the footsteps. Surely this is the finger of God. I am your servant, O Lord. Truly, I am your servant. And my soul says, "You are my Lord."

It must be so. Would you ever put your mark on another's goods? Or would God disown his own workmanship? My name is written in heaven.

You have written your name on my heart, so I cannot question that you have my name on your heart. I have chosen you, O Lord, as my happiness and heritage, and therefore I am sure you have chosen me. For I could not have loved you, unless you loved me first. Amen.

— *Joseph Alleine*

Casting my burdens on Jesus

Most blessed God and Father! I bless you, I praise you, and I desire to love you, in and through Jesus.

And while my whole soul benefits and enjoys the person and work of Jesus, keep me always mindful that it is you, most gracious and almighty Father, that have made him most blessed forever. Your glory is great in his salvation! And the glory of the Son of God is great in your salvation!

Yes, blessed Jesus, I would cast all upon you: sins, sorrows, trials, and temptations. You are the Almighty Burden-bearer of your people, for the Lord has laid on you the iniquity of us all.

And as you bear all our sins, so you carry all our sorrows. And do you not bear every one of your redeemed? Do you not bear all our troubles, temptations, trials, and difficulties? The government is upon your shoulder. The care of the church is all with you.

So will I not cast all my care upon you? Will I worry about many things, while Jesus says, "Cast your burden upon the Lord, and he will sustain you"?

Lord give me grace to let loose all things, and to leave all things with you. Lord, bear me up when I am falling, support me when weak, uphold me against all my enemies, carry me safe through a life of grace here. And, finally, bring me home to your glory, to behold you, and dwell with you forever, amen.

— *Robert Hawker*

I AM COMFORTED WITH HIM

Comfort me with your fruit and your drink, my beloved, and the rest will not matter.

Let your promise be my portion, and your care for my soul. Then whatever is left for my body will be enough.

Lord, let me sit down to eat with you, and I will never complain about the menu. If I have a portion from your table, however much it is, just let me hear your voice saying, "I am yours, and with me are all things." I will be content with your allowance.

With your inheritance in hand, and for my children as well, I ask no more for myself or for them.

I will be quiet and at peace, and I know that all is well. I will not worry, because you are near. Amen.

— *Richard Alleine*

GIVE ME A NEW HEART

My Lord, bring me to the place where you eat. Let me live before your face, let me feel your smiles upon my heart.

Let me love you, and tell me you love me. Remember me. Take pity on me. Accept me. Care for me.

And then choose my condition, my home, and my sources of sustenance.

Give me a new heart, Lord. I am tired. You also are tired of my wicked heart. Make it easier for yourself and for me by taking away this heart—and giving me a better one.

Lord, spread your sweet ointment, let the smell of your garments refresh my soul. Let me taste and see.

Let me see, and I will taste that the Lord is gracious. Amen.

— *Richard Alleine*

YOU HAVE PROMISED GOODNESS

Lord, you are God, and your words are true, and you have promised goodness to your servants.

You have left us nothing to ask from your hands but what you have already freely granted.

Establish forever the word which you have spoken concerning your servants. Do as you have said, and let your name be magnified forever, saying, "The Lord of armies, he is the God of Israel."

Amen. Hallelujah.

— *Richard Alleine*

RUN TO JESUS

Precious, blessed Lord Jesus, let the morning, noon, and evening cry of my heart be in the language of the church of old, and let the cry be awakened by your grace, and answered in your mercy:

"Take me with you! The king has brought me into his chambers! We will be glad and rejoice in you; we will make mention of your love more than of wine" (Song of Solomon 1:4). Amen.

— *Robert Hawker*

WAITING FOR GLORY

Lord, there is but a short life between me and glory, where holy angels and glorified saints will be my associates.

I think I hear already how the morning stars sing together, and all the sons of God shout for joy. O that I could come in!

But I was told to wait, so I will be patient until the end of my days.

It is well, Lord. Your word is enough, and your bond is as good as payment in full.

The Holy Spirit tells me that life and glory await, and that on whatever day I am let loose from the body I will land in paradise.

Amen. It is as I would have it.

— *Richard Alleine*

COME IN YOUR ALL-SUFFICIENCY

Lord, if you have given me Christ, will you not also with him provide everything I need?

Have you given me the fountain, but deny me the stream?

When I beg for pardon of sin, when I beg for power against sin, when I beg for holiness—is all this not granted me in your gift of Christ?

If Christ is mine, is not his blood also mine to secure my pardon? Or his Spirit mine to put down my sins?

If these are all mine, will you withhold them from me?

Will guilt weigh me down, sins live in me, or lusts rule over me—when you have already granted me power for it all to be removed?

Come, Lord. I have too often said, "Depart from me." But if you will not say "Depart" to me, I hope to never again say "Depart" to you.

My misery says "Come." My wants say "Come." My guilt and my sins say "Come." And my soul says "Come."

Come, then, and pardon. Come and convert. Come and teach. Come and sanctify. Come and save me.

Even so, come, Lord Jesus. Amen.

—*Joseph Alleine*

LOOKING FOR THE NEW HEAVENS

Lord, do not be angry that your dust and ashes speak this way to you. But you have raised my expectations, and have made me anticipate great things from you.

If I had not believed, your writing these things to me would have been in vain. Your truth would have been dishonored.

Your words make me repent of my jealousies and my doubtful thoughts about you.

I know you love humble confidence, and delight in nothing more than to see your children trust you. Yet I also know my hopes do not reach a hair's breadth beyond the foundation of your promises. Surely my expectations fall infinitely short of what I will find.

My God, my heart trusts safely in you, and I here confirm that you are true. Christ is the cornerstone on which I build, so my building will stand up to winds and floods.

And now, O Lord, what am I waiting for? My hope is in you. Let me enjoy you fully, and have you in my life. Desire of my eyes, let me see your lovely face and hear your sweet voice.

I only ask what you have promised. You told me that I will see you, and you will clearly speak to me, face to face.

So my knowledge will be perfected. I will see the inaccessible light, and my tender eyes will not water when I look steadfastly at the Sun of Righteousness, to behold your glory.

My faith will be complete and my hope realized. Love will arise like the full moon in her brightness, and never wax nor wane again.

God of my hopes, I look for a new body and a new soul, for new heavens and a new earth, according to your promise. I look for the day when my whole soul will be wholly taken up with you.

All my affections will strain to the highest pitch, and all the wheels of my raised powers set in active and perpetual motion toward you.

And so there will be an everlasting exchange of joy and glory from you, and of love and praise from me. Amen.

— *Richard Alleine*

OPEN OUR EYES, LORD

May that good Spirit of Jesus Christ open the eyes of our minds, that we may see and approve things that are excellent. May he persuade our hearts to receive the truth in the love of it, and direct our steps to walk in the paths of mercy and truth, that we may be saved. Amen.

— *William Ames*

DWELL IN ME, SPIRIT

Lord, if you give me yourself, I will have every gift. If you give me your Spirit, I will have every good thing.

Come, Holy Spirit, and dwell in my soul. I know you will make the place of your feet glorious. If only I have your presence, I will be all glorious within.

Lord, I have heard that Christ is always praying for his people. May I feel the real result of his intercession. May I actually feel his prayers, and the warmth of that spiritual fire which is falling down from his prayers into my heart.

Lord, warm my spirit, and let me feel your kiss, that I may now have communion with you, your spirit upon me, and your protection over me. Seal my pardon, confirm your grace, and save my soul in the day of Jesus. Amen.

— *Isaac Ambrose*

A PRAYER FOR DEPENDENCE ON THE SPIRIT

Lord, may I be more and more under the rich influences and glorious outpourings of the Spirit, that I may be an able minister of the new covenant, not of the letter, but of the Spirit.

I pray that you may always find an everlasting spring and an overflowing fountain within me, which may always make me faithful, constant, and abundant in your work.

May I live daily under those inward teachings of the Spirit that enable me to speak from the heart to the heart, from the conscience to the conscience, and from experience to experience. Let me be a burning and a shining light.

I pray that everlasting arms may be always under me, that while I live, I may be useful for your glory and your people's good, and that no discouragements may keep me from my work.

And when my work is done, help me to give up my account with joy, not with grief. Amen.

— *Thomas Brooks*

Help is in God alone

Lord, I have nothing to move you to show me mercy—
nothing that would convince you to be gracious to me. All
I have would only engage you against me, or shut me out
from mercy.

If sin and unworthiness exclude a sinner from faith and
mercy, I could lie down in sorrow and despair forever.

But it is the glory of mercy to run freely, to flow out upon
those that are most unworthy.

Such am I, Lord, the unworthiest of any who ever sought
faith in you, or that ever found mercy with you.

But the more unworthy, the more will it be for the glory
of your mercy that I not perish. The riches of your grace
appear even greater by your giving me faith.

Glorify your mercy on someone like me. Have mercy on
me, Lord, that I not perish.

Show yourself to be God. Show forth your glory by doing
for me what people and angels, what heaven and earth
cannot do for me.

They all say, while they see me perishing, "If the Lord does
not help you, how will we help?"

I have destroyed myself, but in you alone is my help.

The more helpless my condition, the more will it be for your glory to help me. We hope in vain for salvation from the mountains. And in vain we expect faith from prayers, from ordinances, or from anything else.

Only you can help me to faith.

Help, Lord. All other help is in vain. Amen.

— *David Clarkson*

LET ME HOPE

Blessed Lord Jesus, let the faith of my soul be fixed and unalterable, one that admits neither doubt nor change.

Let me, with full purpose of heart, cling to you, Lord. I see, through your Spirit's teaching, the Father's hand and approval in all your work and finished salvation.

So here let me indeed be fixed, and never be of doubtful mind, but live and die in the full assurance of faith.

Let me be well pleased with what my God and Father is well pleased with, always rejoicing in hope of the glory of God!

— *Robert Hawker*

WHEN YOUR PROMISES KEEP ME

I will not question your faithfulness. If you have said you are my God, should I fear that you are my enemy? If you have told me you are my Father, should I stand aloof, as if I were a stranger?

I will believe, Lord; silence my fears. And as you have given me the claim and title of a child, so give me the confidence of a child.

Let my heart be daily kept alive by your promises, and with this staff let me pass over Jordan.

Turn these promises into my faithful companions and comforters. When I go, let them lead me. When I sleep, let them keep me. When I awake, let them talk with me.

Keep these promises forever upon the thoughts and hearts of your people. Prepare their hearts for you.

And let my heart be the ark of your covenant, where you forever keep and preserve the sacred records of what has passed between you and my soul. Amen.

— *Richard Alleine*

WAITING FOR THE KING OF GLORY

Blessed Lord, my soul rises to you in a flame. You have said you are coming quickly, and I reply, "Amen, even so, come, Lord Jesus!"

Come! I long to be done with the burdens and sorrows of this life.

Come! I long to ascend to your presence, and see you in your courts above.

Death is transformed when I see it in this light. I no longer fear the king of terrors when the King of Glory and Grace is so near.

I hear with pleasure the sound of your feet approaching, nearer and nearer. Draw aside the veil whenever you please.

Open the bars of my prison, so my eager soul may spring forth to you and I may throw myself at your feet—at the feet of Jesus. Though I have not yet seen him, I love him, and I am filled with inexpressible and glorious joy.

Lord, you will show me the path of life, and you will guide me to the place where there is fullness of joy.

You will give me a place with your faithful servants, whose spirits live with you now while their bodies sleep in the dust. Many have been my dear companions in your work, partners in the tribulation and the kingdom, brothers and sisters in Christ.

Blessed Savior, show me how glorious and happy you have made them.

Show me that better life you have given to those we call the dead. Show me how much more noble and busy they are with you, so I can praise you even more for your goodness to them.

I want to share with them in their blessings and service to you, raising a song of grateful love, just like the one they sing in your presence.

Blessed Redeemer, I look forward to that nobler and more glorious hope, and when I am there I will look forward even more to the day of your final appearance. There I will long even more to see you vindicated, your triumph displayed, and the dust of your servants brought back to life. There I will see the final enemy, death itself, swallowed up in victory.

I will long for that greater honor you have reserved for me, and the complete happiness waiting for all your people.

All the millions of your saints, saved by your grace, will say, "Come, Lord Jesus, come quickly!" Their words will mingle with the songs of paradise.

In the meantime, Master, accept the worship and praise my grateful heart offers you now. You have inspired me with glorious hope. You have given me joy, and raised my soul to this place. Otherwise I might have been groveling in the lowest trifles of the here and now, looking with horror to the hour that now excites me so.

Be with me always, even to the end of this mortal life. And
while I await your salvation, help me follow your ways.
Strengthen me and keep my light shining for you.

Keep my ears tuned to the wonderful signal of your arrival,
so my glowing soul springs to meet you with pleasure.
Strengthen and prepare me in death for those visions of
glory which this feeble body could never endure. Amen.

— *Philip Doddridge*

LOOKING FOR THE DAYSTAR

Lord, we commit our souls to your almighty hand. Under
the sanctifying, life-giving, and supporting influences of
your Spirit, help us to wait for your mercy that leads to
eternal life.

Then nothing will sidetrack us—no terror of suffering,
allure of pleasure, or false arguments. But guided by the
light and truth of Scripture, we will march on to your holy
hill.

And when we escape all the dangers of the dark path we
are now on, we will greet the dawn of an everlasting day.

Then we will see the Daystar rise, never to set again.
Amen.

— *Philip Doddridge*

Trusting God in difficult times

O Lord, cast us into whatever dangers you please, and we will cheerfully await the happy event which will at length prove the wisdom and kindness of even your most mysterious plans.

In the meantime, even as we travel in the bonds of affliction, may we see your hand in the expressions and encouragement of our brothers and sisters in Christ.

Like Paul, let us thank you and take courage in the humble assurance that you will stand by us in every future unknown extreme.

You will either display your power and goodness by raising up those around us in support—or you will display your all-sufficiency in a yet more glorious way, bearing us up when everything else fails us. Amen.

— Philip Doddridge

Jesus supplies

Lamb of God! Though you are now in your exalted state, not all the hallelujahs of heaven can keep you one moment from knowing and supplying all the wants of your church in grace here below!

If you ask me, do you have any meat? Lord, I would answer, "You are the bread of life, and the bread of God, the living bread, which comes down from heaven and gives life to the world!"

Precious Jesus! Be my bread, my life, my hope, my fullness, my joy, and my portion forever. Amen.

— *Robert Hawker*

Let the King of Glory come in

Father of spirits, take my heart in your hand. My heart is too hard, and I am too weak. Do not give up on me, though I already have. Just a word from you, in your power, will do the work.

You who have the key of David, you who opens what no person can shut, open this heart and come in, oh King of Glory.

Make this soul your captive. Protect me from the delays of the tempter, until I turn from my sins and accept life on your self-denying terms. Amen.

— *Joseph Alleine*

THE ALMIGHTY BREAKER

Hasten, blessed Jesus! Come, my beloved, and, with a glory infinitely surpassing anything we could imagine, show yourself as the Almighty Breaker, in this full display of your sovereignty and power.

And then, as Samson carried with him the gates of his prison, so will you break up and carry away all the gates of your people's graves, and take all your redeemed home with you to glory—that where you are, there they will be also.

Hail, you Almighty Breaker! Jesus omnipotent, reigns! Amen!

— Robert Hawker

BECAUSE YOU ARE JESUS

Why have I found grace in your eyes? Precious Jesus! The only answer is, because you are—and you will be—Jesus.

Lord, I bow down to the dust of the earth, remembering my vileness and your unspeakable glory. Surely I may look to you, in the opening and close of every day, and every month, as the sure and steadfast anchor of my soul.

You have been to me, and you will always be, what you have been to all your redeemed: a stronghold to the poor, a stronghold to the needy in his distress, a shelter from the storm, and a shade from the heat. Amen.

— Robert Hawker

JESUS MY HIDING PLACE

Dearest Jesus, you are my hiding place. I ask for grace to see you. Surely, from everlasting, in you and in your righteousness, all your redeemed were hidden in peace and salvation.

And when we were called and quickened by grace, what could keep us alive, or preserve our spark from being snuffed out? Only by having our lives hidden with Christ in God.

Yes, blessed Jesus, you are the one who has carried me, as you have said, on eagles' wings, and brought me to yourself. I know that you will never let any of your little ones perish, for "he who touches you touches the apple of his eye."

And while on your wings, whoever wants to destroy them must first destroy you.

So Lord, give me the grace to enjoy and use such amazing blessings. And since you have now added the tenderness and caring of the hen to the wisdom and strength of the eagle, you gather me under your wings.

You nourish me with your love and favor, so I may be yours always, and live here by faith, even as I hope to live with you in glory forever, amen.

— *Robert Hawker*

JESUS MY FRIEND

Do you ask me to set you in my heart, and on my arm?
Lord Jesus, I wish to wear you in my heart. Never, never
depart from my arms.

I wish to feel you inwardly, and to testify to you by every
outward testimony. And as seals upon the arm and upon
the breast are in sight, so I wish to set you always before
me, and tell the whole earth whose I am, and whom I love.

Wherever you go I will go, and where you dwell I will
dwell: for I am no longer my own but am bought with a
price. Therefore I will glorify God in my body, and in my
spirit, which are yours.

Oh precious Lord, when I think of your love and my
ingratitude. ... But Lord, it is yours to love, yours to pity,
yours to pardon.

Lord, give me grace to take you as my own. And while you
are still saying to me, and to your church, "I have called
you friends," may I say, "This is my Friend, and this is my
Beloved, O daughters of Jerusalem!" Amen.

— *Robert Hawker*

THE HEAVENLY SHOW

Precious Lord, may I never watch a show of earthly
pageantry without thinking of your glory. While I watch
the show, however entertaining, help me remember it
is only for today. Let me quickly remember your glory,
which your redeemed will enjoy for all eternity!

Precious Jesus, you are lovely in yourself, lovely in your
cross, lovely in your crown, lovely in all your gracious acts,
victories, triumphs, grace, and mercy.

Everything in you is lovely; and you display that loveliness
to all your people. You have chosen our inheritance for us.
You reign and rule over us, and in us.

You are the Lord our righteousness. Amen.

— *Robert Hawker*

ENLARGE MY HEART SO YOU MAY DWELL THERE

Lord Jesus, your work is to declare the name of the Father
to poor sinners, so you may be in them. Now, Lord, I am
a poor sinner. Declare the name of the Father to me, Lord.
Declare the name of the Father to me.

I have a poverty-stricken heart, without even room
enough for you in my soul. Oh that it were enlarged for
you! So now declare this name of your Father to me, that
the love by which your Father has loved you may be in me,
and I in you also. Amen.

— *William Bridge*

GOD CAN, GOD WILL

Dearest Lord, I blush to think how slender, at times, my faith is!

When I read of the acts of those heroes in the gospel, who "through faith subdued kingdoms, enforced justice, obtained promises, stopped the mouths of lions," and the like, I am ashamed of my unbelieving heart.

Did Joshua bid the sun and moon to stand still? Did Peter call Tabitha from the dead, by faith in Jesus?

And am I so much at a loss, at times, to fear that I will one day perish by the hand of the enemy? I beg you, Lord, strengthen my soul in this grace, that I may never more question your divine faithfulness.

Blessed Jesus, pour in your resources upon my poor forgetful and unbelieving heart, when doubts, fears, and misgivings arise. Help me to see that in all my journey past, you have brought me through difficulties and dangers.

Help me to see that your strength is made perfect in my weakness.

What is difficulty, when Jesus steps in for his people? The challenge, be what it may, is more for the display of your glory, and the exercise of my faith.

Help me then, Lord, to look to you—and not to the difficulty, because I have nothing to do with it. It is enough for me that my God has promised. You can, God, and you will.

How will you do it, Jesus? That is your concern, not mine. You are faithful. You have promised. And that is enough for me. There is no doubt. Yes, Lord! I know your hand is not weak, and all that you have said must come to pass. Because "Faithful is he who calls you, who will also do it." Amen.

— Robert Hawker

MOUNTAINS ARE LEVEL IN GOD'S STRENGTH

Precious Jesus, may it be found that I sat down, counted the cost, and formed my whole plan—but in your strength, and to your praise.

And may it be found that whatever opposition I may meet, like the Tobiahs and Sanballats in the Bible, I may feel the sweetness and encouragement of that blessed Scripture, and say with the prophet:

"Who are you, O great mountain? Before Zerubbabel you shall become a plain; and he shall bring forth the top stone with shoutings of 'Grace, grace to it!'" (Zechariah 4:7). Amen.

— Robert Hawker

JESUS THE ALL IN ALL

Dear and blessed Lord, you are our inheritance and portion forever.

Glorious, gracious, and almighty Father, your choice and your gift confirm, sweeten, and sanctify your eternal and unspeakable mercy.

Holy and blessed Spirit, you cause my poor soul to live by grace here and in glory, to all eternity.

Great, glorious, universal Lord. To you, blessed Jesus, every knee will bow. You are all in all in creation, redemption, providence, grace, and glory. You are all in all in your church, and in the hearts of your people. You are in all our joys, our happiness, our work, our privileges. You are the all in all in your word, ordinances, means of grace. You are the sum and substance of the whole Bible.

Do we speak of promises? You are the first promise in the sacred word, the whole of every promise that follows. You are the "yes and amen."

Do we speak of the law? "You are the end of the law for righteousness to every one who believes."

Do we speak of sacrifices? "By one offering you have perfected forever those who are sanctified."

Do we speak of the prophecies? "To you all the prophets bear witness, that through your name every one who believes on you will receive forgiveness of sins."

Yes, blessed, blessed Jesus, you are the all in all. Be to me, Lord, the all in all I need in time, and then surely you will be my all in all to all eternity, amen.

— Robert Hawker

FOR WHEN WE DOUBT

My Lord and my God, would I cry out, under the same conscious shame of my dreadful unbelief, as Thomas did?

Yes, Lord, you are still ministering, still serving. And though I lose sight of you a thousand and ten thousand times, it is plain and most evident that nothing but your strength could carry me through.

In all the blessings of your finished redemption, you yourself are serving up grace to your people.

You did first purchase all blessings with your blood, and now you live to see them administered by your Spirit.

Precious Jesus, you are ever with me. By and by I will be with you. I will see you as you are, and I will be satisfied when I awake with your likeness. Amen.

— Robert Hawker

YOU HAVE THE WORDS OF ETERNAL LIFE

Father, you have commanded us to pray always, with thanksgiving, and to never stop praying for all the believers.

You have commanded us to continue in prayer, and in everything, by prayer and supplication, to make our requests known to you.

You have directed us to ask, seek, and knock. And you have promised that we will receive, we will find, and it will be opened to us.

You have appointed us a great high priest, in whose name we may come boldly to the throne of grace, that we may find mercy and grace to help in time of need.

You have assured us that while the sacrifice of the wicked is an atrocity, you delight in the prayer of the upright. The praise of the upright glorifies you, and their sacrifice of thanksgiving will please you.

You are the one who hears prayer, so we come to you. You tell us to seek your face, and our hearts answer: we will seek you!

Should a people not seek their God? Where else would we go, but to you? You have the words of eternal life. Amen.

— *Matthew Henry*

MERCY UPON MERCY

Lord, reveal yourself more and more to us in the face of
your Son Jesus Christ.

Magnify the power of grace by cherishing the seeds of that
grace in the midst of our corruption.

Bring us to humility by the way you show us our own sin
and weakness.

And since you have taken us into the covenant of grace,
you will not cast us away, though our sins grieve your
Spirit and remind us how far off we are.

And because Satan tries to obscure the glory of that mercy
through discouragement, add this to the rest of your
mercies:

Since you are so gracious to those who follow you as Lord,
help us not to misuse your grace or lose any part of the
comfort that is laid up for us in Christ.

Let the prevailing power of your Spirit be evidence of the
truth of grace begun in us, a pledge of final victory for
the time when you will be all in all, all yours, for eternity.
Amen.

— Richard Sibbes

OUR SOULS PANT FOR YOU

Who are we, Lord God, that you have brought us here, to present ourselves before you? Who are we, that we have through Christ access by one Spirit to the Father?

What are we, that you are mindful of us? Do not be angry if we take it upon ourselves to speak to the Lord of Glory. We know we are only dust and ashes.

We know we are not worthy to receive the least of your mercies, or all the truth you have showed your servants.

It is not proper to take the children's bread and toss it to people such as we were. Even so, dogs may eat crumbs that fall from their master's table. And you are rich in mercy to all who call upon you.

Whom have we in heaven but you? We desire no one besides you. No one compares to you.

When our flesh and our heart fail, be the strength of our heart and our portion forever. You are the portion of our inheritance in the other world, and of our cup in this world. Our heritage is good.

Our souls desire you in the night, and with our inner spirit we seek you early. As the deer pants for water, so our souls long for you, God. Our souls are thirsty for you, the living God.

You command your lovingkindness during the day, and your song will be with us in the night. And our prayer is that we may come hungering and thirsting to you for righteousness. You fill the hungry with good things, but you send the rich away empty.

I pray that we may thirst for you and long for you in this dry and thirsty land, that we may see your power and your glory—just as we have seen you in your sanctuary. Your lovingkindness is better than life. Our souls will be satisfied, and we will praise you with joyful lips.

We put our trust in you, God. Never let us be ashamed. Truly our souls wait on you, the source of our salvation. You alone are our rock and our salvation. We find in you our glory, our strength, and our refuge. In you, our expectation.

When refuge fails, and no one cares for our souls, we cry to you. You are our refuge, and our portion in the land of the living. Some trust in chariots, and some in horses, but we will remember the name of the Lord our God.

We will trust in your mercy, O God, forever and ever. We will wait on you. We have hoped in your word; remember your word to your servants. Amen.

— *Matthew Henry*

PREPARE MY HEART
FOR THE LORD'S DAY
AND THE LORD'S TABLE.

A SABBATH PRAYER

There can be nothing better than to praise your name,
O Lord, and to declare your lovingkindness in the
morning, on your holy and blessed Sabbath day!

For it is your will and command that we set aside this day
to serve and praise you. We remember with thanks the
creation of the world by the power of your word, and the
redemption of humanity by the death of your Son.

We declare your greatness and power. Yours is the glory
and the victory, and we praise you. Everything in heaven
and earth is yours. Yours is the kingdom, and you excel as
Lord of all. Riches and honor come from you. You reign
over all. You give grace to all. Power and strength are in
your hands.

And as by your mercy you have brought me to the start
of this blessed day, so I ask that you make it a day of
reconciliation between my sinful soul and your divine
majesty. Give me grace to make it a day of repentance
before you. In your goodness, seal it to be a day of pardon
to me.

Help me remember that the keeping holy of this day is a
commandment which your own finger has written, that on
this day I might meditate on the glorious works of creation
and redemption, and learn how to know and keep the rest
of your holy commandments.

And when I meet with other believers to offer you our
sacrifice of praise and prayer, to hear what your Spirit will

speak to us by the preaching of your word, do not let my sins stand as a cloud to stop my prayers from ascending to you, or to keep back your grace from descending by your word into my heart.

May my chief delight be to dedicate myself to your glory and honor, not my own way or my own will. When I cease from my works of sin, as well as the works of my daily calling, may I, through your blessing, feel in my heart the beginning of that eternal Sabbath, which I will celebrate with saints and angels in unspeakable joy and glory, to your praise and worship, in your heavenly kingdom forevermore. Amen.

— Lewis Bayly

PRAYING TO ETERNITY

Precious Jesus, let me go to the place where your people pray. Let me hear your voice, inviting us to be with you.

I will follow the Lamb wherever he goes. I will follow you to the place where your people gather. I will wait to see my God and King in his sanctuary.

My soul thirsts for you, as a deer thirsts for cooling streams. And when I join your people in the place where we pray, may your grace and Holy Spirit fire my soul with a foretaste of that glorious assembly that keeps an eternal Sabbath above—the place where the everlasting praises of God and of the Lamb will grip and fill my raptured soul with joy unspeakable and glory to all eternity. Amen.

— Robert Hawker

BEFORE A SERMON

Lord, I am now entering into your presence, to hear
you speak from heaven to me, to receive your rain and
spiritual dew, which never return in vain, but ripen a
harvest either of corn or weeds, of grace or judgment.

My heart is prepared, O Lord, my heart is prepared
to learn and to love any of your words. Your law is my
counselor; I will be ruled by it. It is my physician; I will be
a patient under it. It is my schoolmaster; I will be obedient
to it.

But who am I that I should promise any service to you?
And who is your minister that he should do any good to
me, without your grace and heavenly call?

Be therefore pleased to reveal your own Spirit to me, and
to work in me that which you require. Amen.

— *Edward Reynolds*

AFTER THE SERMON

Blessed be God, the Father of all mercy, who continues to pour his benefits upon us.

You have chosen and called us, justified us, set us apart, and glorified us.

You were born for us, and you lived and died for us. You have given us blessings for this life, and for a better life to come.

Lord, your blessings hang in clusters, falling upon us. They break forth like mighty waters on every side.

And now, Lord, you have fed us with the bread of life, your word. So we have eaten the food of angels. Bless it, Lord, make it health and strength to us, as we strive and prosper, until our obedience reaches the measure of your love— you who have done everything for us.

Grant this, dear Father, for your Son's sake, our only Savior. With you and the Holy Spirit, three persons, but one most glorious, incomprehensible God, be all honor, glory, and praise forever, amen.

— *George Herbert*

A PRAYER FOR PREPARING A SERMON

Blessed God! You gave me a rational soul, and I depend on you entirely to empower every capacity you have given me.

I am not sufficient in myself; all my sufficiency is of you.

Now I enter this important work, and I want to be aware of my need for your gracious assistance. Keep me focused on the work ahead of me, I beg you. Do not let any vain or intruding thoughts break in or hinder me. Direct my mind to proper thoughts, and to the best way of arranging and expressing them.

Fire my heart with holy affection, that divine thoughts still warm from my own soul may more easily penetrate into the hearts of those who hear me.

Help me remember that I am not speaking to gain a reputation for eloquence, but that I am preparing food for precious and immortal souls, dispensing that sacred gospel which my Redeemer brought from heaven and sealed with his blood.

So direct me to make this sermon most useful for Christian edification. And grant me refreshment as I study, that it may be one of the most joy-filled tasks of my life. While I am watering others, may I be watered myself also, and bring forth daily more and more fruit, to the glory of your great name, through Jesus Christ. Amen.

— *Philip Doddridge*

A PRAYER TO PREPARE FOR COMMUNION

Blessed Lord!

I am grateful you commanded your servants to form themselves into churches—and for the wise and gracious way you have provided for the edification of your church, in holiness and love.

I adore my Savior, who instituted his supper as a memorial of his dying love—a bond of that union he wants his people to preserve through the ages.

Lord, you see how sincerely I give myself to you. And if I now hesitate about this particular manner of doing so, it is not because I would allow myself to break any of your commands, or to refuse any of your favors.

You know any hesitation only comes from uncertainty about my duty—a fear of profaning holy things by an unworthy approach to them.

It is a good sign that you have given me a reverence for your commands, a desire for you, and a willingness to devote myself wholly to serving you. You are inclined to receive me, and believe I am not unqualified for an ordinance which I highly honor and earnestly desire.

So here is my humble request: Would you teach me what I need to do? Show me the way I should take? "Test me, O Lord, and prove me, examine my heart and mind."

Am I hiding any secret sin? Do I make a habit of resisting your precepts? You know that I do not.

So let me not wrong my own soul by avoiding your sacred table for no reason. But grant me this, Lord: may your word, providence, and Spirit together make my way plain.

Scatter my remaining doubts. If you see they have no just foundation, fill me with more assured faith and a stronger love.

Plead your cause with my heart so I cannot delay. If any doubt remains in my mind, replace it with loving concern to avoid whatever displeases your holiness, and then to fully practice what you desire.

May the vision of Christ crucified be so familiar to my mind, and may a sense of his dying love so powerfully motivate me, that I may never question that I am one of those for whom he intended this feast of love!

Even now, joined to your church in spirit and in love—though not as close as I could wish—I pray that you would "save your people, and bless your inheritance; be their shepherd also, and bear them up forever" (Psalm 28:9).

May every Christian church flourish in knowledge, holiness, and love. May all your priests be clothed with salvation, that by them you may make your people joyful.

May many people come to your churches everywhere, flying to them "as a cloud, and as the doves to their windows" (Isaiah 60:8).

May your table be filled with guests (Matthew 22:10), and may all that love your salvation say, "The Lord be magnified, who has pleasure in the prosperity of his servant" (Psalm 35:27).

I earnestly pray that all who have received Christ Jesus the Lord may be careful to walk in him. May we all be prepared for the gathering of your firstborn children.

And may we one day join in a nobler and more immediate worship where all these symbols and shadows will be laid aside—where even these memorials are no longer needed.

Instead, a living and present Redeemer will be the everlasting joy of those who have delighted to commemorate his death in his absence. Amen.

— *Philip Doddridge*

A Communion prayer

How good it is, Lord, to receive a broken Christ into a broken heart. We feed on your body broken, and your blood shed, as the sole, the only, the all-sufficient means of salvation by faith!

Lamb of God! Keep your table sacred from all leaven, both in the persons approaching it, and the offerings made upon it.

Do not allow the leaven of hypocrisy and wickedness here, but let all who meet around your table be of the unleavened bread of sincerity and truth.

And Lord, please come into your house, to your table, to your people. Let each person hear and joyfully accept the invitation of the kind Master: Eat, O friends; drink, yes, drink abundantly, O beloved!

Then Lord, make us yours, altogether yours! Let our whole body, soul, and spirit be all yours, both by the conquests of your grace, as they are justly yours, and by the purchase of your blood.

Never, never more may we depart from you, but as did the church of old, may we exult in this blessed assurance, "My beloved is mine, and I am his." Amen.

— *Robert Hawker*

COME TO THE TABLE

Dear Lord, surely you are the all in all of everything that is sacred and blessed. You are the altar, the sacrificer, and the sacrifice!

And it can only be from your blessing on our poor worship, when we remember your one, all-sufficient sacrifice with a feast, that we discover the deeper spiritual meaning.

Until I hear your call, Lord, I cannot eat. But if you say, "Eat, friends; drink—yes, drink abundantly, beloved," then I feel a confidence in your welcome to every gospel feast. Then I can sit down under your shadow with great delight. Your fruit is sweet to my taste.

Come often to your table, dearest Lord, and sit as a king. Everything at the table is yours: the bread of life, the water of life, and the wine of your banquet.

Come then, dear Lord! Come to your own banquet, to your church, your table, your house of prayer, your ordinances! Come and bless your people! Amen!

— *Robert Hawker*

A PRAYER BEFORE COMMUNION

Holy Lord God, I dare not approach your altar before
I have cleansed my soul by confessing my sins and
professing my faith to you—my only Savior and Redeemer.

You have commanded that I should have no other gods
before you. That I should have my whole delight in you,
and address all my prayers to you, with everlasting praise
and thanksgiving for all I enjoy and hope for.

But I have made a god of this world, delighted in its
vanities and trifles, and preferred them before your
worship and service.

You have commanded that I should make no image to
represent your nature, worship, or incomprehensible
majesty. But I have not worked to pull my mind away
from all visible representations of your majesty, that I
might worship you in spirit and truth. I have not prepared
myself for worship and service as I should.

You have commanded me not to take your name in vain,
but to reverently use your name, attributes, and everything
related to you. But I have abused your name by vainly
mentioning it, your attributes by misapplying them, and
your Scriptures by carelessly reading them. I have not
adorned the gospel with holy and heavenly conversation.

You commanded me to keep holy the Sabbath day. Yet I
have not set it aside to your service, but have been guilty
of worldly thoughts, words, and actions, and have been
careless in my prayers. I have been a hearer and not a doer
of the word.

You have commanded me to honor my father and mother and respect my superiors. But my pride is such that I would if I could cast away every yoke of obedience, and the duties required of me.

You forbid me to kill, and command me to seek to preserve my own life and the life of others. But I have often given way to wrath and revengeful thoughts, and have instead of loving my enemies rejoiced in their misery.

You forbid me to commit adultery, and yet impure thoughts have often possessed me. But as they are sins of darkness, so Lord, I beg you, cover them forever.

You forbid me to steal and command me in the sweat of my brow to eat my bread. But my own heart has been too much set on this world, so I have no thought to gather riches in heaven. You know it to be true, but O Lord, forgive me according to your tender mercies.

You forbid me to bear false witness against my neighbors, and to be careful of their good name. But have I willingly heard them reproached and vilified? Lord, I know you are a God of truth, and hate lying. But has my whole life been nothing but a lie, making a profession of religion, but denying its power?

You forbid me to covet anything that belongs to my neighbor, and to be satisfied with what you have given me. Yet I have secretly murmured when someone else appears to be blessed more than I am. I have not been thankful to you for my portion, though it is more than many of God's dearest children have enjoyed in this world.

And now, Lord, though I have been guilty of several or most of these transgressions, I still have not rent my heart with godly sorrow, nor thoroughly repented of my sins. I have not denied ungodliness and worldly lusts.

Who will deliver me from this body of death? None but you, blessed Redeemer—by the death of your body and by your blood. Now, with the help of your Spirit, I partake in these pledges of your everlasting love, and seals of my eternal redemption.

Wash my hands in purity, and cleanse my mouth by this confession of my sins. Purify me by this profession of my faith in your blood, that with a pure heart I may receive this bread of life.

Give me grace to examine myself thoroughly and sincerely. Fit me with a wedding garment of knowledge, repentance, faith, and love, and show me how to change. Then may I joyfully and thankfully depart from your table. Amen.

— *Robert Parker*

TAKE MY LIFE AND LET
IT BE CONSECRATED.

A PRAYER OF SURRENDER

Who am I, Lord, that I should make any claim on you, or have any part or portion in you, when I am not worthy to lick the dust of your feet?

But since you hold out your mercy to me, and you bid me come, I would be undone to rebel against you in false humility.

So I bow my soul to you. With all possible thankfulness I accept you as my own, and I give myself up to you, my King. You will be sovereign over me, my King and my God. You will be on the throne, and I bow all my strength to you. I will come and worship before your feet. You will be my portion, Lord, and I will rest in you.

You called for my heart. Oh that it were in any way fit for your acceptance! I am unworthy, Lord, everlastingly unworthy to be yours. But since you will have it so, I freely give up my heart to you. Take it; it is yours. Oh that it were better! But Lord, I put it into your hand, who alone can mend it. Mold it after your own heart. Make it as you would have it—humble, heavenly, soft, tender, and flexible. Write your law on it.

Come, Lord Jesus, come quickly. Enter in triumphantly. Take me up to you forever. I give myself up to you. I come to you as the only way to the Father, as the only Mediator, the means God ordained to bring me to God.

I have destroyed myself, but in you is my help. Save, Lord, or I perish. I come to you with a rope about my neck.

I am worthy to die, and to be damned. Never was the wage more due to the worker than death and hell are due to me.

But I fly to your merits. I trust alone the value and virtue of your sacrifice, knowing that you will always intercede for me.

I submit to your teaching, I choose your government over me. Stand open, everlasting doors, that the King of Glory may come in! Amen.

— *Joseph Alleine*

Your will be done

Now speak, Lord, and I will hear. Now call, Lord, and I will answer. Now command me, impose on me what you will, and I will submit.

None but the Lord, none but Christ, no other lord nor lover. I am yours, Lord, your own.

Do with your own, demand of your own, whatever you please.

What will you have me be, Lord, what will you have me do? That is what I will do and be.

No longer what I will, but your will be done. Amen.

— *Richard Alleine*

I GIVE YOU MYSELF

Spirit of the Most High, the Comforter and Sanctifier
of your chosen, come now with all your glory, all your
courtly attendants, your fruits and graces.

Let me be the place you live. I give you what is yours
already. Here, with the poor widow, I cast my two
pennies—my soul and my body—into your treasury. I fully
resign them to you, to be sanctified by you, to be your
servants.

They will be your patients; cure their disease. They will
be your agents; govern every step. I have served the world
too long, and I have listened to Satan too long. But now I
renounce them all. Now I will be ruled by your dictates
and directions, and guided by your counsel.

Blessed Trinity! Glorious unity! I deliver up myself to you.
Receive me, write your name on me, and on everything I
have. Set your mark on me, on every member of my body,
and every part of my soul.

I have chosen your ways and your law. Now I will keep
it in my view. By your grace, I resolve to walk in your
way. I will be governed by your law. And though I cannot
perfectly keep one of your commandments, I will not
allow myself to disobey any.

I know my flesh will hang back. But in the power of your
grace, I resolve to cleave to you and your holy ways—
whatever the cost.

With you I am sure I will never lose. So I will be content with disapproval, difficulties, and hardships. I will deny myself, take up my cross, and follow you.

Lord Jesus, your yoke is easy and your cross is welcome, since it is the way to you. I lay aside all hopes of worldly happiness. I will be content to wait, and come to you. Let me be poor and low, little and despised here—so I may live and reign with you hereafter.

Lord, you have my heart in this agreement, never to be reversed. By grace I will stand in this resolution, where I will live and die. I have sworn that I will keep your righteous judgments. I have freely made my everlasting choice.

Lord Jesus, confirm the contract. Amen.

— *Joseph Alleine*

A PRAYER OF SELF-DEDICATION

Eternal and ever-blessed God! I humbly present myself before you.

I am aware how unworthy a sinner like me appears before the holy Majesty of heaven, the King of kings and Lord of lords.

But here I dedicate myself, without reserve, to you.

This is your plan. You stooped down to offer it by your Son, and your grace has inclined my heart to accept. I say "God, be merciful to me, a sinner!"

I come, invited in the name of your Son, wholly trusting in his perfect righteousness. For his sake be merciful, and remember my sins no more.

Receive me, I beg you. I am convinced of your right to me, and desire nothing more than to be yours.

Today I solemnly surrender myself to you. I renounce all former lords that had dominion over me.

I consecrate to you all that I am, and all that I have: my mind, body, possessions, time, and influence over others.

I dedicate all to be used entirely for your glory, in obedience to your command, as long as you give me life.

I desire to continue with you through endless ages of eternity. I will stand ready to immediately follow your will with zeal and joy.

I resign myself—all I am and have—for you to use in your infinite wisdom, however you choose, for your glory.

I leave the management of my life to you. I say without reservation, "Not my will, but yours, be done." And I rejoice in your unlimited government.

Use me, Lord, as an instrument of your service. Number me among your chosen people. Wash me in the blood of your dear Son. Clothe me with his righteousness and sanctify me by his Spirit.

Transform me more and more into the image of Christ. Impart to me all the influences I need of your purifying, cheering, and comforting Spirit. Let me spend my life under those influences, in the light of your countenance.

And when the hour of death comes, may I remember your covenant, "ordered in all things, and secure"—grant me "all my salvation, and all my desire" (2 Samuel 23:5).

Though every hope and enjoyment perish, Lord, look down with pity on your child. Embrace me in your everlasting arms.

Put strength and confidence into my departing spirit, as I peacefully and joyfully await the fulfillment of your promise to your people—a glorious resurrection and eternal happiness in your heavenly presence.

And if any surviving friends should, when I am in the dust, come across this memorial of my transaction with you, may they make it their own. Allow them to take part in the blessings of your covenant, through Jesus the great Mediator.

To him, and with you, O Father, and your Holy Spirit, be everlasting praise from all the millions you save, and from the celestial spirits whose work and blessings you share! Amen.

— *Philip Doddridge*

DRAW ME CLOSER, IN YOUR TIME

Can such a heart be worth having? Make it so, Lord, and then it is yours. Take it to yourself, and then take me.

Like a feeble child to a tender mother I look up to you and stretch out my hands. I long to have you take them.

You know I am not weary of your work. I am willing to stay while you here employ me. I dare not be so impatient of living, as to beg you to cut off my time. Nor would I stay when my work is done, and remain under your feet.

I am content, Lord, to wait for your time, and go your way, if you will take me into your barn when you see that I am ripe.

I am content to wait, but not to lose you. Quicken my dull desires, and blow on the dying spark of love. Do not leave me until I can sincerely cry out, *As the deer pants for water, so I long for you, O God. I thirst for God, the living God. Where can I find him to come and stand before him?*

Draw forth my soul to yourself by the secret power of your love, as the sunshine in the spring draws creatures from their winter homes. Meet it halfway, draw me to yourself, like a compass is drawn to the north.

Dispel the clouds that hide your love from me, or remove the scales that keep my eyes from beholding you. For only the beams that stream from your face, and the taste of your salvation, can make a soul say, *Lord, now let your servant depart in peace.* Amen.

— *Richard Baxter*

WE HAVE OBTAINED GRACE TO GIVE OURSELVES TO YOU

We have obtained grace to give ourselves to you, Lord, through your mercy, and to one another.

To have communion with one another, as saints in one gospel fellowship, we agree and promise before God the Father and our Lord Jesus Christ to walk together in this one gospel communion and fellowship as a church of Jesus Christ.

In love to the Lord and to one another, we endeavor to give sincere and hearty obedience to the laws, ordinances, and appointments of our Lord and lawgiver in his church.

We also agree and promise, the Lord assisting, to follow after the things which make for peace, and things with which we may build each other up.

So living and walking in love and peace, the God of love and peace may be with us. Amen.

— *John Bunyan*

MAKE ME USEFUL AGAIN

You are the bountiful Father and sovereign Author of all good, whether natural or spiritual.

I bless you for the talents with which you have enriched me, and which I do not deserve.

But my soul is in shambles before you when I consider how little I have put them to good use.

Compared to what you might reasonably have expected, what have I done with all the gifts you bestowed—the abilities, time, talents, possessions, and influence?

Through my own negligence and foolishness, the only result is a barren wilderness, where I might have seen a fruitful field and abundant harvest!

I deserve to be stripped of everything and brought to immediate account—condemned for unfaithfulness to you, to the world, and to my own soul. I ought to be cast into the prison of eternal darkness.

But you, Lord, have freely forgiven the dreadful debt of ten thousand talents. I adore you for this.

Accept my renewed surrender, Lord. I again submit myself and all that I have to serve you. I admit that I give you only what is your own to begin with (1 Chronicles 29:14).

Make me a faithful steward for my great Lord, I beg you. And do not let me consider my own interests, those opposing yours.

I adore you, God of all grace! Let me feel a love for others rise in my soul. Open my heart so I may reach out to serve.

Help me to be fair and thankful in determining what is my own share—the portion you intend for me and my family. For the rest, help me to faithfully, cheerfully, and wisely distribute your bounty to those who need it most.

Guide my hand, ever-merciful Father! I am honored to be your instrument.

And if it is your gracious will, would you also multiply the seed sown (2 Corinthians 9:10) and prosper me in order that I may have even more to give to those in need?

And then would you lead me on to the place of unlimited plenty and compassion, where I may see many that I had helped on earth. And—if it is your will—also many of those whom I introduced to saving faith.

They will entertain me in their home of glory!

In time and eternity, Lord, accept the praise of all, through Jesus Christ—at whose feet I would bow.

And in the end, after I have run my course, I will die at his feet, worshiping him then with sincere humility and gratitude as if for the first time. Amen.

— *Philip Doddridge*

A NEW PASSION TO FOLLOW GOD

Do what you will with us, God. We are your servants!
Give us life and support, and the weakest of your children
will not stumble at the greatest of your promises on
account of unbelief. Strong in faith, we will give you glory.

Lift up our affections to higher and nobler things than
what our lowest human nature pursues. Teach us to
completely control our bodies, that we would not be cast
away from your presence or fall into that horrible place
where every ounce of sinful pleasure will be paid for with
pounds of misery and despair.

Send your Spirit fully into our hearts, Lord, and teach us
to cry "Abba, Father!" As children, draw us to yourself
with reverence and confidence. Show us how to love each
other, even the family of God you so graciously lead.

Inspire us with that zeal for your glory which will make
the honor of your name, the good of your kingdom, and
the accomplishment of your will far dearer to us than any
interest of our own.

Help us to cheerfully depend on you for our daily needs,
and let us be content with the food and clothes you
provide.

Help us also to seek your forgiveness for past sins, and
give us grace to preserve us from future temptations, or to
secure us and protect us in them.

May that sense of our own need for your forgiveness drive us to forgive each other, especially since you have wisely and graciously made this the avenue for receiving our own pardon.

Our corrupt hearts are not inclined this way. But may your almighty power produce in us a new desire, even passion to forgive. And while the comfort is ours may all the glory be yours, through Jesus Christ our Lord. Amen.

— *Philip Doddridge*

AM I BEING CHANGED INTO CHRIST'S IMAGE?

Unless I am born again, I cannot enter heaven.

Born again? What does that mean, Lord? Did that kind of thing ever really happen to me? Was I ever cast into the pangs of a new birth? And did those pangs of new birth continue until Christ Jesus was formed in me?

Are old things done away, so that all things have become new?

Is the old person, the old lusts, the old way of speaking, totally abandoned? Have they been left behind?

Are my principles made new? My goals? My life? Amen.

— *Isaac Ambrose*

A PRAYER OF SURRENDER

Lord, I yield. I am overcome; O blessed conquest!

Go on victoriously, and still prevail, and triumph in your love. This captive of love will proclaim your victory when you lead me in triumph from earth to heaven, from death to life, from the tribunal to the throne.

I will acknowledge that you have prevailed, and all will say, *Behold, how he loved him!*

Let neither life nor death, nor anything separate me from your love! Keep me in the fullness of love forever, amen.

— *Richard Baxter*

I LAY MYSELF AT YOUR FEET

Lord, I am under no bonds that ought to bind me, or that justly can, against your sovereign right.

Other bonds took a place in my heart and the affections of my soul—but they were bonds of sin, which I regret I ever made.

I thought I was my own, and I lived to myself. I only pleased and served myself, as if I were created for no other reason.

And while I pleased myself with imagined liberty and self-dominion, no idol was too despicable for me to worship. My soul bowed down to a clod of clay. My thoughts and desires, hopes and joys, all stooped to trifles: wealth, ease, pleasure, fame.

And while I thought I was free, I was a servant to corruption. What have I done, Lord? I have lived to myself, and not to you. I have been a stranger to you. I will through your grace be so no longer.

But now, Lord, through your mercy, I have learned to abandon myself. Your grace appeared and taught me to deny ungodliness and worldly lusts. You have overcome: enjoy your conquest.

I am sorry that you had to contend for and conquer your own. I repent.

So Lord, I here lay myself, and all that belongs to me, entirely at your feet. All things are of you, and I bring them to you in a willing, joyful offering. What I have in the world is more yours than mine.

I desire neither to use nor possess anything without it being for your sake and by your permission.

Flow in with all the mighty powers of your own love upon my soul. You who can raise up children from stones, and make them the true, genuine sons of Abraham—and there can be no such children, without love—dissolve this stone, this stone that is my breast.

Soften this stubborn heart, and turn it into love, amen!

—*John Howe*

MY AMEN TO YOUR AMEN

Lord! Lay whatever burden you will upon me, only let your everlasting arms be under me.

Strike, Lord, and do not spare me. I lay down in your will. I have learned to say amen to your amen.

You have a greater interest in me than I have in myself, and therefore I give myself up to you. I am willing to be at your disposal, and am ready to receive whatever impression you want to stamp upon me.

Blessed Lord, again and again you have said to me, as once the king of Israel said to the king of Syria, "I am yours, and all that I have" (1 Kings 20:4).

I am yours!

Your mercy is mine to pardon me.

Your blood is mine to cleanse me.

Your merits are mine to justify me.

Your righteousness is mine to clothe me.

Your Spirit is mine to lead me.

Your grace is mine to enrich me.

And your glory is mine to reward me.

Therefore my soul cannot help but resign myself to you.

Lord! Here I am; do with me as seems good in your own eyes.

I know the best way to have my own will is to resign myself to your will, and to say amen to your amen.

— *Thomas Brooks*

MAKE MY HEART THE GOOD GROUND

I know, O Lord, and tremble to think, that three parts of the good seed fell upon bad ground.

Let not my heart be like the highway. Through hardness and want of true understanding it does not receive the seed, so the evil one comes and takes it away.

Let not my heart be like the stony ground, which hears with joy for a time, but falls away as soon as persecution arises for the gospel's sake.

Let not my heart be like the thorny ground, which chokes the word and makes it altogether unfruitful because of the cares of this world and the deceit of riches.

Let my heart be like the good ground. Help me to hear your word with an honest and good heart. Enable me to understand and keep it, and bring forth fruit with patience, for your glory and my everlasting benefit. Amen.

— *Lewis Bayly*

FOLLOWING JESUS, ALL DAY LONG

Blessed God! You are the great fountain of being and of happiness.

Just as my being came from you, so my happiness flows directly from you. And the nearer I am to you, the purer and more delicious the stream.

With you is the fountain of life; in your light may I see light (Psalm 36:9)!

The great object of my final hope is to dwell forever with you. Give me now a foretaste of that delight. Help me to experience the blessedness of one who fears the Lord, who greatly delights in his commandments (Psalm 112:1).

Form my heart by your grace, that I may live in the fear of the Lord all day long (Proverbs 23:17).

I direct my awakening thoughts to you, Lord. And with the first ray of light that visits my opening eyes, lift up the light of your countenance on me (Psalm 4:6).

May my first actions when I awake be consecrated to you, O God. You are the one who gives me light, life, and a new reason to live.

Enable my heart to pour itself out before you as your child, with reverence, freedom, and endearment. And may I listen to you, as I desire that you would listen to me.

May I read your word with attention and pleasure. Shape my soul into its mold, and may I hide it in my heart that I may not sin against you (Psalm 119:111).

Help me to renew my dedication to you each morning, through Jesus Christ your beloved Son—and from him receive new supplies of your blessed Spirit, whose influence is the life of my soul.

With that preparation, Lord, lead me by the hand into the day. Help me to abide with you in what you have called me to do (1 Corinthians 7:20), not being slothful in zeal, but fervent in spirit, serving the Lord (Romans 12:11).

May I know the value of time, and always use it wisely in whatever work you assign me. Whether I eat, or drink, or whatever I do, may it always be to your glory (1 Corinthians 10:31).

May every refreshment and release from my work prepare me to serve you with greater energy and resolve.

And when afflictions come—which I expect in this world— may I remember that they come from you. And may that understanding fully reconcile me to them.

Because the same love which gives us our daily bread also gives us our daily crosses. Teach me to take them up, and follow you, Lord (Mark 8:34), with the same attitude you showed while climbing to Calvary for my sake. Help me to say, as you did, "Shall I not drink the cup that the Father has given me?" (John 18:11).

And when I enter into temptation, Lord, deliver me from evil (Matthew 6:13).

Make me aware of my own weakness, that you may strengthen me as needed.

While I am with others, help me to do and receive as much good as possible, looking to my life's greatest purpose by honoring you in everything.

And when I am alone, help me always to remember that my Heavenly Father is with me. Help me to enjoy your presence and power as it awakens me to think and act in your sight.

So let me spend my days, ending them always in the fear of God and under a sense of your gracious presence.

Meet me in the evening, Lord. Help me to choose the best time for regular reading and prayer, and to look at my devotion as you do.

Do not let me deceive myself, but let me judge myself as one who expects God to judge. I want to be approved by you, the one who searches all hearts.

Let my prayer come before you as incense, and let the lifting up of my hands be like the morning and the evening sacrifice (Psalm 141:2).

May I fall asleep in sweet serenity, knowing I have lived to God this day, convinced that I am accepted in Christ Jesus my Lord, and humbly trusting in your mercy through him—whether I live many more years or not.

If death comes upon me slowly, may it find me busy in your service. And if I am called on to suddenly exchange worlds, may I still be living my life to please you.

Either way, may I have a sweet and easy passage from the services of time to the infinitely nobler services of an immortal state.

I ask it through him, who, while on earth, was the best example of every virtue and grace, and who now lives and reigns with you, always able to save (Hebrews 7:25).

Having done all, I will fly to him with the humble acknowledgment that I am an "unworthy servant" (Luke 17:10).

To him be glory forever and ever. Amen.

— *Philip Doddridge*

ERRING ON THE SIDE OF LOVE

O Lord, let your grace and your love do for us what fear of your terrors alone cannot.

Melt our hearts by that nobler principle, and teach us to despise everything that would displease you.

Let our hearts respond with the same kind of compassion that motivated you, Jesus, to serve the poor.

And whenever we do make mistakes, let us err on the side of compassion—a love that would never harm the worst sinner—much less the least and weakest of God's servants.

We consecrate our lives to you, Lord, even to death. We will not then feel the bitterness of death half so much, when our hearts are ablaze with a zeal for your glory.

Amen.

— *Philip Doddridge*

BE THE LORD OF MY HEART

Precious Lord Jesus! You, and you alone, give life,
purity, and sweetness to our poor persons and offerings.
Everything in us is corrupt, and we decay. But in you, and
by you, as the manna was preserved, we are preserved.
We are made clean and holy in your holiness and purity.

You are still the bread of God, the living bread, which
that manna represented. You still feed your church above,

and lead them to fountains of living waters. And surely, Lord, you will no less feed your church below, which yet remains in this dry and barren wilderness, where there is no water.

I hear what the Spirit says to the churches, and I feel delight: "To the one who overcomes I will give some of the hidden manna."

Precious Jesus! May my soul always look to you as my faithful, everlasting, unchangeable high priest. "Send forth your mighty scepter from Zion! Rule in the midst of your enemies!"

I am sure, Lord, that everything in me and from me will remain dry. So I look to you for life and grace to my poor soul, to bring forth fruit—by your grace and for your eternal glory.

Sovereign Lord! Almighty King! I gladly acknowledge you as my King and my God. I by the appointment of God, by your conquest of my heart, and by my voluntary surrender since you brought me under the power of your grace, am yours, and no longer my own.

Oh, for grace to acknowledge you, to obey you, to love you. And as the Father has set you upon your throne, may his grace also give you the throne of my heart! And while all your enemies must bow before you, may all your friends and followers rejoice in your service! Even so, Amen!

— *Robert Hawker*

WE WILL WALK IN YOUR WAYS

Lord, our souls have told you: you are our God.

Other lords have had dominion over us, but we affirm the Lord this day to be our God.

We will walk in your ways, keep your commandments, honor your judgments. We will listen to your voice and give ourselves to you as your people—for your praise, and for your glory.

Lord, truly we are your servants, born in your house. You have loosed our bonds. We are bought with a price, so we are not our own, but yield ourselves to you. We join ourselves to you in an everlasting covenant that will never be forgotten.

We are yours. Save us, for we seek your ways. We give you what is yours, that which comes from your hand. Amen.

— *Matthew Henry*

No will but yours

Jesus, it is my aim divine, hence to have no will but yours.
Let me covenant with you, yours forevermore to be.
This my prayer, and this alone:
Savior, let your will be done!
You to love, to live to you: this my daily portion be.
Nothing to my Lord I give, but from him I must first receive.
Lord, for me your blood was spilled.
Lead me, guide me, as you will.
All that is opposed to you, however dear it be,
From my heart the idol tear.
You shall have no rival there.
Only you will fill the throne.
Savior, let your will be done.
Will you, Lord, in me fulfill
All the pleasure of your will.
Yours in life, and yours in death.
Yours in every fleeting breath.
You my hope and joy alone.
Savior, let your will be done.

— *Octavius Winslow*

CROWNING THE KING

With what humble confidence may a poor sinner, such as I am, look up and tell him of the glories of his cross, now shining in the glories of his crown!

Will I not hope, dear Lord, by the sweet influence of your blessed Spirit, to make every day a coronation day, when by faith I crown you my true and lawful sovereign?

I desire to bring every thought and affection of my poor heart into obedience to you. I want to bow the knee of my heart before you, and with holy joy confess that Jesus Christ is Lord, to the glory of God the Father. Amen.

— *Robert Hawker*

I AM HIS

Lord, grant me grace to abide in Jesus, that every act of my life may testify whose I am, and whom I serve.

And like the martyr who answered every question "I am a Christian," may my every thought, word, and action proclaim Jesus and my union and oneness with him—so that everyone may plainly see I am no longer my own.

But instead, being "bought with a price, glorify God with your body." Amen.

— *Robert Hawker*

I WILL CLING TO YOU

From eternity, Lord, did you entertain thoughts of glorifying me, a miserable wretch? I am less than nothing.

I will carry you forever in my eyes, and always in my heart. I will delight in meditating on you.

I will cry out, "How precious are your thoughts to me, O God! How vast is the sum of them!" (Psalm 139:17).

With true repentance, I regret all the hours, days, weeks, months, and years that have passed without one single holy and pleasing thought of you.

Did you, out of mere love, choose me to salvation? Then I will choose you for my Lord, my King, for the portion of my soul, for my chief—or rather, my only—delight.

Did you choose me from among so many others, who, left to themselves, face eternal destruction?

I will make every effort to surpass others in love, in your worship, and in all the duties of holiness.

You predestinated me to holiness, which is so lovely in itself, and so necessary for me. Without it, there can be no salvation. And I will walk in it, never separating the end from the means. Was only the end predestinated, in neglect of the means, to which I was no less predestinated?

Your purpose for my salvation is fixed and unchangeable. So why would I change every hour — at one time giving my service to you, and another time to the devil?

I will cling to you. And I would sooner choose a thousand deaths than forsake or betray you. I will be steadfast, immovable, always abounding in the work of the Lord, for I know my labor will not be in vain (1 Corinthians 15:58).

By your spirit, you draw me to your love, which passes all understanding. And I will love you again with all my heart, mind, and strength.

You give me the assurance of my salvation. And with this hope, I will purify myself, as you are pure (1 John 3:3).

Lord, honor me, in a way so extraordinary and undeserved, that you take me for your child. You declare this to me by spreading your love in my heart by the Holy Spirit you have given me.

And I will love, worship, honor, and obey you to the utmost of my power. Let me be emptied of everything else, that I might be filled only with your love! Amen.

— *Herman Witsius*

YOUR NAME ON MY HEART AND HOME

Precious Jesus, you have been a strength to my poor soul, and you will be my portion forever. Help me to see my daily need of you, and to feel my poverty and weakness.

From persecution to my guilty conscience, to the remains of sin in a body of death, to the accusations of Satan or even the just judgments of God—I am secure in you, Lord Jesus. And I continually cry out, as did your prophet: "Only in the Lord … is righteousness and strength; even to him shall men come." I will never be ashamed or confounded, world without end.

You have given grace, glory, and honor to your Israel. I want your name, Lord, on the gates of my house, so that no one will walk by and miss the fact that a lover of the Lord lives there!

It is my highest honor to have it known whose I am, and whom I serve, in the gospel of his dear Son. How could I be ashamed of that name before which every knee bows in heaven and on earth?

And Lord Jesus, not only write your name upon the gates of my house, but engrave it in the center of my heart and my affections—on my first, and last, my earliest, and latest thoughts!

Let it be my joy to speak out of the abundance of my heart about you and your great salvation. In all I say, in all I do, let it be clear that I am in pursuit of the one my soul loves.

Let my every action point to your dear name. And whether at home or abroad, in my house or family, when lying down or when rising up, let all creation witness for me, that the love, the service, the interest, the glory of my God in Christ is the only object of my soul's desire.

Let every thing in my life say this: "Whom have I in heaven but you? And there is none upon earth that I desire besides you. My flesh and my heart may fail; but God is the strength of my heart and my portion for ever." Amen.

— *Robert Hawker*

I WANT TO BE YOURS

Lord, you are as worthy to be the Omega as you are the Alpha. The last as you are the first. The end as you are the beginning of all things. The ocean into which all being will flow, as the fountain from which it sprang.

I cannot live except by you. You are God alone. You are the fullness of life and being, the only root and spring of life, the everlasting I AM, the Being of beings.

You know all things. You know that I love you, and because I do, I present myself to you. It is all I can do.

I wish myself ten thousand times better, for your sake. And if I had in me all the excellencies of many thousand angels, it would not be enough. Nothing but your own goodness could make me worthy of your acceptance.

Because I love you, I want to be near you. I want to be yours. I want to lead my life with you, to dwell in your presence. I love you, O Lord, my strength, because your own perfections highly deserve it—and because you have heard my voice. You have delivered my soul from death, my eyes from tears, and my feet from falling.

My only resort, O Lord, is to your mercy. You might most justly abhor and abandon us, and say to us, "Lo-ammi, for you are not my people."

But in the multitude of your tender compassion and mercy, do it not.

Lord, here I am, wholly yours. I come to surrender myself, my whole life and being, to be entirely and always at your disposal, and for your use. Accept a devoted, self-resigning soul.

I have here brought you back a stray, a wandering creature—my own self. I heard what the Redeemer has done and suffered to reconcile us. Against your known design, I can no longer withhold myself from your plan for me.

And I yield myself to you, because I love you. I make an offer of myself to be your servant—your servant, O Lord. You have loosed my bonds, and now I desire to bind myself in new ones to you, that are never to be loosed. Amen.

—*John Howe*

A PRAYER OF DEDICATION

With trust and hope I commit my spirit into the hands of Jesus my glorified Redeemer and Intercessor—and through his work into the hands of God my reconciled Father.

You are infinite eternal Spirit, light, life, and love. You are most great and wise and good. You are the God of nature, grace, and glory, of whom and through whom and to whom are all things.

You are my absolute owner, ruler, and benefactor; whose I am, and whom I serve, seek, and trust—though imperfectly.

To you be glory forever, amen.

— *Richard Baxter*

HELP ME GIVE THE
GOSPEL TO OTHERS.

GOD ALONE CAN SAVE

O Lord, how insufficient I am for this work. With what will I pierce the scales of Leviathan—or make my heart, hard as a millstone, feel what you desire it to feel?

Will I go and speak to the grave, and expect the dead to obey me and come forth?

Will I make a speech to the rocks, or lecture the mountains, and move them with arguments?

Will I make the blind see?

From the beginning of the world no one has ever heard of opening the eyes of a person born blind. But, Lord, you can pierce the heart of the sinner.

I can draw the bow at random, but you direct the arrow between the cracks of the armor.

I come in the name of the Lord of Hosts, the God of the armies of Israel. I come forth, like David against Goliath, to wrestle, not with flesh and blood, but with rulers and cosmic powers, and spiritual forces of evil of this world.

This day let the Lord defeat the Philistines, take away the armor from the strong man, and give me the captives out of his hand.

Lord, choose my words. Choose my weapons for me. And when I put my hand into the bag, and take out a stone and sling it, and carry it to the mark, make it sink—not into the forehead, but into the heart of the unconverted sinner.

Take him to the ground like Saul of Tarsus.

Lord God, help! How can I leave them this way? If they will not hear me, still I pray that you will hear me. I pray that they might live in your sight! Lord, save them, or they perish.

My heart would melt to see their houses on fire when they were fast asleep in their beds. So is my soul moved within me to see them endlessly lost?

Lord, have compassion, and save them out of the burning. Put forth your divine power, and the work will be done.

Slay the sin, and save the soul of the sinner. Amen.

— *Joseph Alleine*

O Lord, draw people to Christ!

For those who do not know you yet, Lord, grab on to them now, and do your work. Take them by the heart, overcome them, and persuade them, until they say, "You have won. You are stronger than I."

Lord, did you not make me a fisher of men? I have worked all this time and caught nothing. Have I spent my strength for nothing?

I will cast my net one more time. Lord Jesus, stand on the shore and show me how and where to spread my net. Give me the words to enclose the souls I seek, that they will have no way out.

Now, Lord, for a multitude of souls. Now for a full portion.

Lord God, remember me, I pray, and strengthen me, O God. Amen.

— Joseph Alleine

NOW IS THE DAY OF SALVATION

Blessed Jesus, you have done all this, and more. You are the door into your fold here below, and to your courts above. For you have said that by you, "Whoever enters in will go in and find pasture."

And you have opened a new and living way by your blood. You are the only possible way of access to the Father. And because you have opened it, no one can shut it. You live to keep the way you once opened, still open, by your continuing intercession.

Heavenly Lord, the gate is never shut, day nor night. In the preaching of your everlasting gospel, all the ends of the earth will see this salvation of our God. And, as you have graciously said, all that come to God by you, will never be shut out.

The word has gone out. Your blood and righteousness secure it. The Spirit sets his seal to it. You will receive, you will bless, you will cause all the Father has given you to come to you. And you will keep the door always open for all comers.

What a precious, endless salvation! I pray that my fellow sinners, still outside, would rouse up from their carnal security and sloth, before the master of the house gets up and shuts the door.

"Now is the acceptable time; behold, now is the day of salvation." Amen.

— *Robert Hawker*

A SALVATION PRAYER

Lord, I am a lost and fallen creature by nature and by actual transgressions beyond number, which I confess to you this day.

I have lived without you, senseless and ignorant. But you have impressed on my heart how miserable I am in myself, and have shown me the remedy provided by Christ Jesus.

You have offered him freely to me, on the condition that I would accept this offer and flee to Jesus. And now you have sovereignly determined my heart, and formed it for Christ, causing me to approach the living God.

Therefore I am here today to settle the matter, according to your will. Unworthy as I am, I declare that I believe that Christ Jesus, slain at Jerusalem, was the Son of God, the Savior of the world.

I believe there is eternal life in Christ, and in Christ alone. I trust my soul to you, Jesus. I accept God's reconciliation through you. I choose you in all that you are. I submit all that I am, or have, to you, and divorce myself from everything you hate—without reservation or exception, and no turning back.

Here I give my hand to you. I accept God's offer of peace through Christ, and make a covenant with you today, never to be reversed. Subdue my corruption. I place my neck under your sweet yoke in all things, and cheerfully submit my heart to whatever you want to do to me, or with me.

Now I give you praise, Father, for devising this salvation, and for giving it to the Son to accomplish.

I give you praise, Jesus, who paid such a dear price, and through whom I have access to the Father, in whom I am reconciled and united with God. I am no longer an enemy or a stranger.

I give you praise, Holy Spirit, for sounding the alarm when I was destroying myself, for convincing me that I was in danger, for opening my eyes to the remedy, and for persuading my wicked heart to fall in love with Jesus. Now you are teaching me how to covenant with God. You are showing me the sure mercies of David and the blessings of Abraham, and how to secure the favor and friendship of God forever.

I submit my choice this day with my heart, head, soul, and whole person. I resolve not to be my own, but yours. Whatever concerns me will be on you, as my head and Lord. Failings on my part (against which I resolve, as you know) will not make void this covenant.

For so you have said, and I intend not to abuse your mercy, but so much the more to cling close to you. I have liberty to renew and ratify this transaction, as often as needed.

I know your consent to this bargain stands recorded in Scripture, so I need no new sign. I accept your offer on your terms. You are faithful and you will pardon whatever is lacking in my way of doing this.

God is true, and Jesus saves. Amen.

— *William Guthrie*

A PRAYER FOR MY NEIGHBORHOOD

May God's grace visit all who suffer loss, and may your compassionate eye regard them where they live.

May your providence cement, strengthen, and adorn them. For unless the Lord builds the city, they labor in vain who build it.

May the candle of the Lord shine on them, and your Spirit enlighten and renew their souls. May peace and prosperity, friendship and faith always flourish in this neighborhood and city.

Fill my neighbors' troubles with compassion, Lord, so they may exchange joy for mourning, and beauty for ashes. So that those who lament may rejoice with you, and that at length you may share with them the security and joy of the city of God, the heavenly Jerusalem, where no flames will be felt except those of love.

In the meantime, may our eyes be lifted up to heaven, in the humble hope and fervent prayer for those around us, that true Christian faith would spread throughout the entire world. And may that faith prevail in our own hearts, that we may faithfully practice and grow in you.

So will we understand your lovingkindness, Lord, as we live our daily lives. And though there may be mysteries of providence we cannot explain, we will believe that your

paths are mercy and truth, and find the truest and securest
peace in our passage to everlasting joy. Amen.

— *Philip Doddridge*

FATHER, CURE THE WORLD'S DISEASE

Great eternal Original, Author of all created beings and
happiness: I adore you—you who have made us capable of
faith. You who have bestowed this dignity and eloquence
on our nature, that it may be taught to say, "Where is God
our Maker?"

But I lament that degeneracy has spread over the whole
human race, which has turned our glory into shame. The
forgetfulness of God, unnatural as it is, has become a
common and universal disease.

Holy Father, we know that only your presence and
teaching can reclaim your wandering children. Impress a
sense of divine things on the heart, and make that sense
lasting and effectual.

From you proceed all good purposes and desires—and
this desire, above all, of spreading wisdom, piety, and
happiness in this world.

Though we are sunk in such deep apostasy, your infinite
mercy has not utterly forsaken us. Amen.

— *Philip Doddridge*

INVITE THE STRANGER IN

Wonderful Stranger, did you come from a far country, on
this gracious, blessed errand to seek and save that which
was lost?

And did you find every heart firmly shut against you?

Jesus, when you traveled in the greatness of your strength,
did you open an entrance into the souls of your people, by
the sweet influence of your Holy Spirit?

Then throw open the street doors of my heart! Make
them like the gates of that blessed city, never shut by
day or night. And cause my soul, like the prophet on the
watchtower, or Abraham in the tent door, to be always
on the lookout for my Lord's approach. In this way I may
invite you, even beg you to come in and abide with me.

Make yourself known to me by the heart-burning discourses
of your word, and in breaking of bread and of prayer.

Yes, glorious Traveler! I do know you, and I sometimes
catch a sweet glimpse of you, and trace the footsteps of
your grace—in your word, in your ordinances, and in the
ways by which we can discover your presence.

Heavenly Stranger, you are not going to sleep in the street;
I will take you home to my house, to my heart and soul.
As you promised, you will eat with me, and I with you.

But Lord, while I share your bounty, help me always
to remember where it comes from. And while I eat and

drink, Lord, send portions to them for whom nothing is prepared.

We pray for your presence to be always in view at every supper, and the savor of your name to be like an ointment poured forth.

By your Spirit, direct our conversation to build up others, so we may talk of Jesus, while Jesus draws closer to us. At every supper, remind us of the supper of the Lord.

By faith, we will enjoy that marriage supper of the Lamb in heaven—at which we hope, before long, to sit down forever. Amen.

— *Robert Hawker*

HELP OUR WITNESS

Lord, we profess the faith, and yet care not for the dying.

We profess, and yet long not for the coming of the day of God.

We profess, and yet by our whole life show to them that can see how little a measure of it we have in our hearts.

Lord, lead us more into the power of things. Then the virtues of him who has saved us, and called us out of darkness into his marvelous light, will be made known to others. Amen.

— *John Bunyan*

FOR THE SPREAD OF THE WORD

Almighty and ever-living Lord God: majesty, power, brightness, and glory!

How will we dare to appear before your face, we who are contrary to you? For we are darkness, weakness, filthiness, and shame. Yet you are our Creator, and we your work. Your hands made us. You placed us in paradise—until we sold our glorious, gracious God for an apple.

Brand it on our foreheads forever: For an apple we once lost our God, and still we lose him for nothing more. For money. For food.

But you, Lord, are patience and pity. Sweetness and love. Therefore we are not consumed. You have exalted your mercy above all things. You have made our salvation our glory, not our punishment.

Where sin abounded, grace super-abounded—not death. When we had sinned beyond any help in heaven or earth, you said, "See, I come!"

The Lord of life took flesh. He wept; he died. For his enemies he died, even for those that derided him then, and still despise him.

Blessed Savior! Many waters could not quench your love! No pit could overwhelm it. Though the streams of your blood carried through darkness, grave, and hell, yet you rose triumphant, and so made us victorious.

But your love does not stay here. For you have committed the word of your rich peace and reconciliation not to thunder or angels, but to weak and sinful people.

Blessed be the God of heaven and earth, who only does wondrous things. Awake all my powers to glorify you! We praise you! We bless you! We magnify you forever!

And now, O Lord, we stand in the power of your victories, in the way of your ordinances, and in the truth of your love.

Bless your word, wherever it is spoken today throughout the universal church. Make it a word of power and peace, to convert those who are not yet yours, and to confirm those who are.

Bless your word in this your own kingdom, which you have made a land of light, a storehouse of your treasures and mercies.

Do not let our foolish and unworthy hearts rob us of your sweet love, but pardon our sins, and perfect what you have begun.

Ride on, Lord! Make your word a swift word, passing from the ear to the heart, from the heart to the life. As the rain returns not empty, so may your word accomplish that for which it is given.

O Lord, hear. O Lord, forgive! O Lord, listen. For your blessed Son's sake, amen.

— *George Herbert*

SHOW YOURSELF TO THE NATIONS

Reach out your mighty arm, O Lord God, show your strength in the sight of all the nations.

Spread your salvation on the hearts of multitudes, that they may believe and turn to you.

May the great Savior of Israel be found by those who seek you not, and through the surprising condescension of your grace, show yourself to those who do not inquire of you.

May your ancient people not only be provoked to anger, but awakened to follow the same path, and put in their claim for those blessings which you by your Son have stooped low to offer all the Gentiles. Amen.

— Philip Doddridge

FORGIVE MY SINS.

Cleanse me, Emmanuel

Dear Emmanuel, in whom alone, and by whom alone, all my hopes and confidences are founded: I fall down at your feet.

As the prophet cried out, so I desire unceasingly to exclaim, "I am a man of unclean lips!"

But if you cause the iniquity to be taken away, and my sin to be purged from me, I will be clean. For you are our New Testament altar.

You are the Lord my righteousness. Precious Jesus, you are the Alpha and Omega.

Even as the Father made you the glorious covenant head of your people in the beginning of his way, so be my all in all. My first and last. The Author and Finisher of my faith.

Precious Lord! May I, like Paul, be able to say, "Not that I have already reached the goal"—because I long to catch up to and hold fast to you, Christ Jesus, even as you have caught up to and held fast to me.

So come, Lord Jesus, to your bride, the church. Be the fountain of life to all your redeemed, until you bring your church below to join your church above, so they will dwell together in the light of your countenance, forever, amen.

— *Robert Hawker*

MY SINS! MY SINS!

My heart is a sin-pool; I cannot even count the swarms of sinful thoughts, words, and actions that have flowed from it.

My head and my heart are full from the load of guilt that is on my soul. My mind and body are full of sin.

My sins, they stare at me! My creditors are upon me. Every commandment takes hold of me, for more than ten thousand talents, yes, ten thousand times ten thousand.

How endless then is the sum of all my debts! If this whole world were filled up from earth to heaven with paper, and all this paper written over by mathematicians, yet, when all were added up, it would still fall inconceivably short of what I owe to the least of God's commandments.

For my debts are infinite, and my sins are increased. They are wrongs to an infinite Majesty.

And if one who commits treason here on earth is worthy to be punished, what have I deserved—someone who has so often lifted up my hand against heaven, and have struck at the crown and dignity of the Almighty?

It would be better to have all the regiments of hell come against me than to have my sins fall upon me. Lord, I am surrounded!

The sands are many, but then they are not great. The mountains are great, but then they are not many.

But my sins are as many as the sands, and as mighty as the mountains. Their weight is greater than their number.

It would be better that the rocks and the mountains fall upon me, than that the crushing and unsupportable load of my own sins would remain.

If my grief were thoroughly weighed, and my sins laid in the balance together, they would be heavier than the sand of the sea.

O Lord, you know my mighty sins. They have brought nothing but misery. What a mess I am in! I am sold as a slave to sin, cast out of your favor, cursed in my body, and cursed in my soul. I am cursed in my name, in my relations, and in all that I have.

My soul is within a step of death.

What do I do? Where will I go? Which way will I look? Where should I flee? What place could hide me from your presence, everywhere? What could secure me from your unlimited power?

Will I linger any longer like this, the way I was? No. If I waited there as I was, I would die.

What then? Is there no help? No hope? None, unless I turn.

But is there any remedy for such woeful misery? Any mercy?

Yes! As sure as your promise is true, God, I will have pardon and mercy—if I now genuinely, and without reservation, turn by Christ to you.

So I thank you on the bended knees of my soul, O most merciful Lord, that your patience has waited for me. Because if I had died as I was before, I would have perished forever.

And now I adore your grace, and accept the offer of your mercy.

I renounce all my sins, and resolve by your grace to set myself against them, and to follow you in holiness and righteousness all the days of my life. Amen.

— *Joseph Alleine*

IN HUMILITY

Dearest Lord Jesus, I blush when I think of how your glory was veiled in humiliation; and then I compare it to how often my poor fallen nature has been hurt by some imagined, trivial offense.

I desire the same attitude as yours, Jesus, when you humbled yourself. Amen.

— *Robert Hawker*

HELP ME CRY, LORD

I mourn, Lord, and I lament. I weep, but it is because I cannot mourn or lament as I should.

If I could mourn as I ought, I would be comforted. If I could weep, I would rejoice. If I could sigh, I would sing. If I could lament, I would live.

But I die. I die, and my heart dies within me, because I cannot cry. I cry, Lord, but not for sin. I cry, I beg for tears for sin. I cry, Lord—my calamities cry, my bones cry, my soul cries, my sins cry, "Lord, for a broken heart."

But look: I am not broken yet.

The rocks tear apart, the earth quakes, the heavens drop, the clouds weep, the sun will blush, the moon be ashamed, the foundations of the earth will tremble at the presence of the Lord.

But this heart neither breaks nor trembles. If only I had a broken heart! If I did, you would have your way in my heart. What would be impossible, if my heart were tender?

Work would be easy. Pains would be a pleasure. Burdens would be light.

Neither the commands nor the cross would be severe. Nothing would be hard except sin.

Where are you, fear? Come and plough up this rock.
Where are you, love? Come and thaw this ice, come and
warm this dead lump, come and enlarge this poverty-
stricken spirit.

Then I will run in the way of your commandments.

I accept of all that is yours, both your yoke and your cross.
I accept you, Lord—your love, and whatever you will.

Lord, if you love, let me love you. I will seek until I can
see. Let me see, until I can love.

What do I have here, Lord? My all is with you: my help,
my hope, my treasure. My life is hidden with Christ in
God. Yet this is all nothing to me, while my heart is not
with you.

Take it, Lord, take it up. Where my treasure is, there let
my heart be also. Amen.

— *Richard Alleine*

I AM THE ONE TO BLAME

What had you done, my Savior, that Judas betrayed you, and you were led, bound as a lamb to the slaughter? What evil did you commit, to be falsely accused and unjustly condemned? What was your offense? Whom did you ever wrong, to be scourged with whips, crowned with thorns, reviled, buffeted, and beaten?

Oh Lord, how did you deserve to be spit upon, covered with shame? To have your garments parted and your hands and feet nailed to a cross? To be lifted upon the cursed tree, to be crucified among thieves? To endure such a sea of God's wrath, that made you cry out, as if you had been forsaken by God your Father? To have your innocent heart pierced with a cruel spear, and your innocent blood spilled before your mother's eyes?

I can find no offense in you. The centurion who executed you confessed you to be the very Son of God. The thief that hung with you said you had done nothing wrong.

So what caused this cruel disgrace, suffering, and death?

Lord, I caused your sorrows. My sin brought about your shame, my failings your injuries. I committed the fault, and you are plagued for the offense. I am guilty, and you are charged. I sinned, and you suffered the death. You hung on the cross.

Oh the deepness of God's love, the wonder of his grace! Mercy without measure! What can I say?

I was proud; you are humble. I was disobedient; you
became obedient. I ate the forbidden fruit; you hung on
the cursed tree.

O Lord, let me never forget your infinite love. Amen.

— Lewis Bayly

LIGHT UP MY CONSCIENCE

Make me understand, Lord, where I have gone wrong.
Make me recognize my transgression and my sin. Search
me and try me, and then enable me to search and try
myself—with fairness, over and over.

Remove whatever might make me blind, or narrow, or
distracted.

Light up and awaken my conscience. It is your officer, so
let it be your voice to faithfully represent your charges
against me.

Direct others and bless your word, that it may be a
searching, convincing light.

Bring it all together, that I may understand when you
contend with me, and with your people, and with these
nations. Amen.

— David Clarkson

PRAYER OF A CONVICTED SINNER

Injured King and almighty Judge, what can I say to the charges against me? Should I pretend to be offended, and defend myself? I do not dare. You know my foolishness. None of my sins is hidden from you.

My conscience tells me that denying my crimes would only increase them, and add new fuel to the fire of wrath I deserve.

I am more guilty than I can say. My heart speaks more than any accuser. And you, Lord, are much greater than my heart. You know it all.

What has my life been but rebellion against you? It is not this or that particular sin alone. From start to finish, nothing has been right. My whole soul has been disordered.

All my thoughts and affections, my desires, my pursuits— everything has been alienated from you.

I have acted as if I hated you—you who are infinitely the loveliest of all beings. As if I had been trying to wear out your wonderful patience.

My actions have been evil, my words yet more so. And my heart, how much more corrupt than either!

What a fountain of sin and original corruption is my heart. It mingled its bitter streams with the days of early childhood, and flows on even to this day. And I have been growing worse and worse, provoking your patience more and more.

I am astonished that your patience continues. If the offense were against me, I could not have endured it as you have. Had I been a prince, I would long since have done justice on any rebel whose crimes even faintly resembled mine. Had I been a parent, I would have long since cast off such an ungrateful child.

Why then, Lord, am I not cast out from your presence? Why am I not sealed up under an irreversible sentence of destruction! I owe my life to your indulgence.

But if there is yet any way of deliverance, any hope for so guilty a creature, may it be opened to me by your gospel and grace.

If any more humiliation or terror is needed for my salvation, may I bear it all! Wound my heart, Lord, so you can afterward heal it. Break it in pieces, if you will bind it up in the end. Amen.

— *Philip Doddridge*

MARVELOUS GRACE ON CORRUPT SINNERS

Lord, how dull and remiss I am in the practice of my duty to you. You have said, "Cursed is the one who does the work of the Lord negligently" (Jeremiah 48:10). Then what do I deserve? There is no surprise that I feel no power. I deal with you and listen to you halfheartedly. My prayers are cold.

Lord, you love a cheerful giver, but my service is maimed, corrupt, dead, superficial, and uncheerful.

Lord, I have slighted your promises. I have neglected the motions of your Holy Spirit. I have not carefully cultivated the gifts I have received, and I have not labored more and more to be sealed with the promised Holy Spirit. Ah, Lord, how miniscule is my holiness! Because of my laziness, your grace is held back.

Lord, you have looked on my poor condition, and you have visited me with mercy from on high. Though I was a stranger and a foreigner, you have made me a free citizen of the new Jerusalem.

Now I see, and I read it in your precious promises, that my name is registered in heaven. An eternal weight of glory is reserved for me. Heaven is my home, my hope, my inheritance.

Where is my heart? With my treasure! I cannot comprehend your love and favor, dear Lord! What kind of mercy is this? What kind of promises? My soul rejoices in you, my God, and my spirit will bless your name forever and ever, amen.

— *Isaac Ambrose*

DISCIPLINE ME

My Lord, give me your rod and staff. If my disease overtakes me, give me a stronger cure. If my reckless heart will not be tamed, put more restraints on me—load upon load, weight upon weight.

Let me never be sick of your remedy until I am cured of my disease. Let me rather suffer by the hand of a demon than perish from lust.

Do not spare me, Lord. Do not hold back from disciplining your servant, until by doing so you have struck down all my enemies.

Peace, plenty, leisure ... to spend on my lusts, to rebel against my God? I do not want that kind of peace. I would rather have pain and trouble or be in need—anything rather than peace on those terms.

Correct me, God, but only in your judgment, not in your fury. Otherwise I would be consumed and brought to nothing. Amen.

— *Richard Alleine*

IT ALL BELONGS TO JESUS

Precious Jesus! I do remember my faults this day. So grant me from now on to live wholly to you, gracious Lord, to keep you always in view, walking with you, cleaving to you, hanging upon you. Help me always to remember you and your love more than anything else.

You, my dearest Redeemer! I pray for grace to set you always before me, to record in my heart your mercies, and to set you in my heart. To follow you wherever you go, and to watch the steps of Jesus. To pursue you in all your paths, at your table, at your ordinances, in your words, in your house of prayer, in your providence, in your promises.

Everywhere, and in all things, where Jesus is, I pray that there may my soul be. Though I have no way to pay you back for this bounty, Lord, still in your grace may I follow you, to bless you, and to live out the truth that all I am and all I have is yours.

Grant me in this sweet sense to know you, precious Jesus, and to enjoy you in everything, for riches and honor come from you.

Yes, Lord, the work is yours, salvation is yours, glory is yours—everything is yours. All that remains for me is to be forever giving you the praise that is due your most holy name, content to be nothing—even less than nothing—that the power of Jesus may rest on me. Because when I am most weak in myself, then am I most strong in you, Lord, and in your power, amen.

— *Robert Hawker*

THE PRAYER OF A CONDEMNED CRIMINAL

I am reduced to a horrible condition. I have sinned, and what can I say to you, God?

I was a fool to amuse myself with petty excuses, and to imagine they would carry any weight in your presence.

Now I am silent. My hopes are dead. I am almost ready to wish that my immortal soul could die, too.

I am a criminal in the hands of justice, disarmed, stripped of the weapons I once trusted.

Now I can expect nothing other than condemnation from you. I know you have recorded it in your word, that your intention was gracious—that you want to alarm us, not destroy us.

Speak to me, God! I know it is a fearful thing to fall into the hands of the living God. And in one sense I have already fallen into your hands. So whatever your sentence is, I must condemn myself and justify you. Amen.

— *Philip Doddridge*

WE ARE ASHAMED

We are ashamed, Lord, and we blush to lift up our faces before you.

Our sins increase over our head, and our trespasses rise up to the heavens. To us belong shame and confusion, because we have sinned against you.

How can we answer you? If it would help, we would lay our hands on our mouths, put our mouths in the dust, and cry "Unclean! Unclean!" with the leper under the law.

When our eyes have seen the King, the Lord of Hosts, we have reason to cry out, "Woe to us, for we are undone!"

Dominion and fear are with you. You are a consuming fire; who knows the power of your anger?

Who may stand in your sight when once you are angry? If we try to justify ourselves, our own mouths will condemn us. You, who are greater than our hearts, know all things.

We ourselves know that we have sinned, Father, against heaven and before you, and are no more worthy to be called your children.

But there is forgiveness, mercy, and redemption with you. You will not despise a broken and a contrite heart, though you are the High and Lofty One that inhabits eternity, whose name is holy.

Though heaven is your throne, and the earth your footstool, still you will look to the poor and humble person who trembles at your word. You revive the spirit of the humble, and the heart of the contrite.

The ones who cover their sins will not prosper, yet those that confess and forsake them will find mercy. You have said that if we confess our sins, you are faithful and just to forgive us our sins, and to cleanse us from all unrighteousness. Amen.

— *Matthew Henry*

HELP ME PRAISE AND
THANK THE LORD.

A WONDERFUL, LOPSIDED TRADE

What is left, O Lord, but to spend the rest of my days loving, praising, and admiring you?

But how can I come before the Lord, or bring myself before the most high God? What can I give you to express my thankfulness, a poor exchange for your bounty?

What a shame that my soul is so poor, and so weak. A shame that my voice can reach no higher a note of praise! But will I do nothing, because I cannot do all?

Lord, I yield my all to you. With the poor widow, I cast my two pennies, my soul and body, into your treasury. All my powers will love and serve you. Everything in me will be weapons of righteousness for you.

I lay all at your feet. There you have them; they are yours. My children I enter as your servants. My possessions I give up as your right. I will call nothing mine but you. Everything that is mine is yours.

I can say, "My Lord and my God," and that is enough. I thankfully give up my claim to everything else. I will never again say, "My house is mine," or "My wealth is mine."

I myself am not my own.

It is infinitely better for me to be yours, than if I were mine own. This is my happiness, that I can say, "My own God, my own Father."

And what a blessed exchange have you made with me: to give me yourself, an infinite sum, for myself, a mere nothing!

And now, Lord, accept and own my claim. I am not worthy of anything of yours—much less of you. But since I have a deed to show, I bring your word in my hand and am bold to take possession. Amen.

— *Richard Alleine*

JESUS THE BUYER AND THE SELLER

You, Lord, are too rich to need anything from your creatures, and you have yourself already bought the most costly things with a price no less dear than your own most precious blood.

So my wise, gracious, kind, and compassionate Lord, I pray for grace to accept your counsel, and to buy from you gold tried in the fire, the white clothes of your righteousness, and the anointing of your blessed Spirit. Without money and without price.

I need them all, amen.

— *Robert Hawker*

MY THANKFUL HEART WITH GLORYING TONGUE

My thankful heart with glorying tongue
Will celebrate your name,
Who has restored, redeemed, re-cured
From sickness, death, and pain.
I cried; you seemed to take some pause,
I sought more earnestly.
And in due time you supported me,
And sent me help from high.
Lord, while my fleeting time still lasts,
Your goodness let me tell.
And new experience I have gained,
My future doubts repel.
A humble, faithful life, O Lord,
Forever let me walk;
Let my obedience testify,
My praise lies not in talk.
Accept, O Lord, my simple gift,
For more I cannot give;
What you bestow I will restore,
For of your alms I live.

— *Anne Bradstreet*

OVERWHELMED BY YOUR GRACE

O Lord, I bless you, not only for your pardon of those
sins I have committed, but also for your goodness in
preserving me from those many thousands of other sins I
was prone to fall into.

If I could repent to the highest degree, or achieve the
holiness of men and angels, it could not make up the
damage sin has made upon me.

Who was more plunged into sin than I? Whose diseases
were greater than mine? It may be that thousands and
thousands of other souls are now taking their place in hell,
for less and fewer sins than I have committed.

I do not call upon you to repeal any threat or nullify
your word. I do not ask you to become unjust. But your
wisdom has found out a way that I may be pardoned and
you may be satisfied.

Your overflowing goodness overcomes me. If only I had
the hearts of all men and angels to praise you. Amen.

— Anthony Burgess

I AM FOREVER SECURE

Lord, today you have set before me out of your word a glorious mystery—a righteousness of your Son that I did not know or care about before.

I see now my happiness lies there. No matter what happens to me in the world, and no matter what happens to my name or my worldly possessions, I am forever secure if I have Christ to clothe me.

Lord, if righteousness did prevail, then you would be honored more than ever. We would have the joy of our hearts, we would be delivered from the temptations we encounter, and your saints would not suffer as they do. Amen.

—*Jeremiah Burroughs*

LONGING FOR HIS GLORY

Blessed Jesus! We can add nothing to you, nothing to your glory, but it is a joy of heart to us that you are what you are, that you are so gloriously exalted at the right hand of God.

We long more fully and clearly to behold that glory, according to your prayer and promise. Amen.

—*John Owen*

SUCH A GREAT RANSOM

As often as we are tempted to run from serving you, Lord, let us remember the price with which we are bought.

How great a price, the thought of which fills us even with secret shame—as well as admiration and love.

Lord, you have paid such a ransom for me! Shall I now act as if I thought it was not enough? As if you had acquired only a partial and imperfect right to me, so I might divide myself between you and strangers, between you and your enemies?

May we be entirely yours! And may we make it our business, even on the very last day and hour of our lives, to glorify you with our bodies and with our spirits, which are yours.

Lord, we await your salvation. And in the meantime, we will follow your commands. Filled with life by so exalted a hope, we will purify ourselves, even as you are pure. Amen!

— *Philip Doddridge*

YOU ARE GOD ALONE

My God, what can I say to you—except that I love you more than words can express?

I love you for what you are to all your creatures. In all their forms and every moment, they owe their life and happiness to you. It is far beyond what my narrow imagination can conceive, but everything they know is from you.

But I adore and love you far more for what you are in yourself.

Even after creating so much, your reserves of perfection remain untouched, and can never be used up. Your infinite perfection makes you your own happiness.

You are your own end. You are worthy of a respect that never depends on anything outside yourself.

You are first, most beautiful, and only. Greatest and only great.

Possess all my soul! And surely you do possess it.

While I feel your sacred Spirit breathing on my heart, causing me to love you, I also feel the reality of this human, animal life.

If ever I knew the appetite of hunger, my soul hungers after righteousness—and longs to be more like you (Matthew 5:6).

If ever I felt thirst, so also my soul thirsts for the living God—and pants for more of your favor (Psalm 42:2).

If ever I have longed for my bed after a long journey, my soul rests on your grace—and returns for rest in your embrace (Psalm 116:7).

And if ever I have enjoyed seeing the face of a friend, I rejoice in seeing your face, O Lord—and in calling you my Father in Christ.

That is who you are, and that is who you will be, for time and for eternity. What more can I do, but commit myself to you for both?

I leave it to you to choose my inheritance and order my affairs (Psalm 47:4). My only business is to serve you, and all my delight is to praise you.

My soul follows hard after you, God, because your right hand upholds me (Psalm 63:8). Let it still bear me up, and I will press on toward you, until all my desires are fulfilled in the eternal enjoyment of you! Amen.

— *Philip Doddridge*

WHERE PRAISE GROWS TO PRAYER

Precious God, precious Jesus! What a love is here.

O for grace, for love, for life, for every gift of my God and Savior. O that my lips would praise you constantly and unceasingly, forever, as the drops of the honeycomb which follow each other—sweetly and freely, from the abundance of my heart, not constrained, except in the constraint of your love.

I pray that prayer would follow praise, and praise grow into prayer. That there may be a movement to magnify and adore the riches of your grace. That the name of Jesus may be always in my mouth—from that one blessed source, that Jesus lives in my heart, and rules, and reigns, and is formed there in the hope of glory.

Blessed Jesus, you are the one your people will praise. You are the next of kin, the nearest of all relations, and the dearest of all relatives. And by your blood you have redeemed both soul and body, both lands and inheritance. You have redeemed the whole, never more to be lost or forfeited.

And now, Lord, your jubilee trumpet sounds, and the everlasting gospel is heard in our land, to give liberty to the captive, sight to the blind, to bring the prisoners out of the prison, and them that sit in darkness out of prison.

Make me know the joyful sound, and daily walk in the light of your countenance. Cause me, by the sweet influence of your Spirit, to live in the constant expectation of the year of the everlasting jubilee—when the trumpet of the archangel will finally sound, and all your redeemed return to Zion with songs and everlasting joy.

Your people will obtain joy and gladness, and sorrow and sighing will flee away.

Hallelujah! Amen!

— Robert Hawker

YOU OUT-DO YOUR GRACE

What will we say in return for the knowledge you have already given us, for the love you have already wrought in our hearts, if we are so happy as to know your grace in truth?

Even as we believe your power to out-do all that grace has already given us, to do for us exceeding abundantly above all we can ask or think, we will still confide in you and call upon you.

And we will humbly endeavor to do our part with the whole church in ascribing to you, our Redeemer, our Sanctifier, and our Father, glory throughout all ages, world without end. Amen.

— Philip Doddridge

BLESSED ARE THE POOR

Is it not so much better that the people of Jesus are what they are, that they may be better suited for your glory, and that their wants may give an opportunity for grace?

Almighty Sovereign! If I were always poor, needy, or feeling my nothingness, it would motivate me to come to you. Every day's necessities would offer a fresh chance to crown you Lord of all in a day of grace, until I come to crown you, with the whole church, the everlasting Lord of all in heaven, to the glory of God the Father.

Almighty Father! Let my poor soul ever praise you, love you, obey you, and adore you. I praise you that you have fulfilled this covenant promise to your dear Son. And you have indeed subdued the natural stubbornness of my nature, and made me willing to be saved, your way.

And now, blessed Lord, I want to bend the knee of my heart to Jesus, and every day, every hour, ascribe the whole of my salvation "to Him who sits on the throne, and to the Lamb that was slain, forever!"

Blessed Jesus, what is it now but your favor that secures me in your love, and gives me inexpressible mercy, pardon, and peace now, and everlasting glory hereafter? Is not your favor better than life? Is it not more precious than rubies? Can there be anything better?

Truly, Lord, in you and your favor I have life, for you are both my light and my life. My heart trusts in you. Remember me then, Lord, with the favor that you give your people. Visit me with your salvation, amen.

— *Robert Hawker*

THE EVERLASTING SONG

Blessed Lord Jesus! We know the redemption of your church was your one great goal and plan. You went forth before time began. In time, when you came in our flesh, still your goal was the salvation of your people.

And now in eternity, you are still going forth, in your priestly office on your throne, which you continue in heaven for the same purpose: to secure the salvation of your people.

I pray for grace to always remember. And while, in one eternal act, you always are moving for the salvation of your redeemed, may we also go forth in love, adoration, and praise. Help us to acknowledge your mystery, and begin here on earth the song which is never to end in heaven:

Unto him that loveth us, and loosed us from our sins by his blood; and he made us to be a kingdom, to be priests unto his God and Father; to him be the glory and the dominion for ever and ever. Amen.

— *Robert Hawker*

GLORY TO THE ASCENDED ONE

Risen and exalted Jesus, send down your ascension gifts.
Or better, come down yourself and dwell among us. Set
up your church in the earth, and in the hearts and souls of
your people. Reign and rule here, Lord of life and glory.

Jesus, you are the glorious vine of your church. Cause
me to be so united to you, as a branch in you, the one
heavenly plant your Father has planted, that in you my
fruit may be found.

I pray that I may always receive a fresh word from you,
that I may live upon you, and to you, and rejoice in you.
You are the source and fountain of all that is gracious here,
and the everlasting spring of glory, happiness, and joy
hereafter.

Precious Lord Jesus! Take away all remaining darkness,
ignorance, unbelief, and whatever comes in the way of
seeing you clearly, or enjoying you. And let the covering
which is cast over all people, and the darkness over all
faces, be removed for the full enjoyment of you, in grace
here and in glory to all eternity, amen.

— *Robert Hawker*

MY PRAISE FLOWS TO YOUR OCEAN

Lord Jesus! I ask for grace to seek you, as I would for hidden treasure. I want to seek you, and you alone, O my God!

I want to separate myself from all other things. My soul chooses Jesus. My soul needs Jesus. I want to trust in nothing else.

Not duties, not works. Neither prayers nor repentance. Not even faith itself, as an act of my soul, will be my comfort.

But in Jesus alone, I make you my center. Every thought, every affection, and every desire, like so many streams meeting in one. They should all pour themselves, as rivers, into the ocean of your bosom!

And the nearer, as a stream that draws near the sea is propelled to fall into it, so the more forcible and intense let my soul be in its desires for you—even as my soul draws nearer to the hour of seeing you.

Oh Lamb of God, help me to seek you through life, pressing after you from one worship service to the next. And when those cease, and all outward comforts fail, then, Lord, may I gather up (as the dying patriarch did his feet in the bed) all my strength, and pour my whole soul into your arms, crying out, "I have waited for your salvation, O Lord!" Amen.

— *Robert Hawker*

Risen Lord, eternal priest

Precious Lord, you are the one who was dead but now lives forevermore.

And you will live to see the fruits of your great salvation faithfully and fully applied to every one of your redeemed. Your priesthood is forever, your intercession unceasing.

I behold you, Lord, by faith. Even now you stand with the blood of the covenant in your hand. And you present me— poor, wretched, worthless me—as one who was purchased by this blood.

I hear your voice in those soul-reviving words, "Holy Father, keep them in your name whom you have given me, that they may be one, even as we are."

Oh glorious, gracious, almighty High Priest, you are indeed a priest forever, after the order of Melchizedek.

Precious Jesus! You are more and more precious as my soul longs for you more and more. Help me to see that everything in me and from me is but dung and dross. But accept both me and my poor offerings, and let both be sweetly sanctified and perfumed with the incense of your blood and righteousness!

Lord, may you be my whole and sole perfection for righteousness here below, and may I be found "perfect in Christ Jesus" in a life of grace, that I may everlastingly enjoy you in a life of glory hereafter. Amen.

— *Robert Hawker*

WELCOME TO THE WEDDING FEAST

Precious Lord Jesus, clothe me with the wedding garment
of your righteousness, and feed me with the rich food of
your body and blood.

Be my covering, my joy, and my all—so that when I am at
your church, at your table, at your house of prayer below,
or at your kingdom of glory above, you the King will come
in to see your guests, and my soul may cry out.

I will say, in your own blessed words, and with a joy
unspeakable and full of glory:

"I will greatly rejoice in the Lord! My soul shall be joyful
in my God! For he has clothed me with the garments
of salvation! He has covered me with the robe of
righteousness, as a bridegroom adorns himself with a
garland, and as a bride adorns herself with her jewels."
Amen.

— *Robert Hawker*

Counting God's Glory

Holy, holy, holy. Lord God Almighty, who is, and was, and is to come.

O you, whose name alone is Yahweh, and who is the Most High over all the earth.

O God, you are our God, early will we seek you. Our God, we will praise you; our fathers' God, we will exalt you.

O you, who are the true God, the living God, the one only living and true God, and the everlasting King; the Lord our God, who is one Lord.

You are very great. You are clothed with honor and majesty. You cover yourself with light as with a garment. You are light, and in you is no darkness at all.

You are love, and they that dwell in love dwell in God, and God in them.

You are the Father of light, with whom is no variableness or shadow of turning, and from whom proceeds every good and every perfect gift.

You are the blessed and only ruler, the King of kings, and the Lord of lords, who only has immortality, dwelling in the light which no one can approach, whom no one has seen or can see. Amen.

— *Matthew Henry*

WHO IS OUR PRAISE BUT JESUS?

Who will be our praise but you, Jesus—your beauty, your
glory, and your excellence? You are the one in whom all
divine perfection is focused.

Who will be our praise but Jesus, the Mediator, the Christ
of God, whose glory it is to redeem poor sinners and
make them saints, to give out of your fullness, and grace
for grace?

Who will be our praise, but you who have made our peace,
in the blood of your cross, and ever lives to intercede
for us?

Fair and lovely one, the first among ten thousand, you are
my praise, my glory, my song, my rejoicing!

I will praise you every day; morning by morning will
I praise your name, and night by night testify to your
faithfulness.

Here, while I am on the earth, will I never stop speaking
of your praise. And before long, I will join the happy
multitude above, in that song: "To him who has loved us,
and washed us from our sins in his own blood!"

Jesus, you are the praise of all the saints. Amen.

— *Robert Hawker*

THE GLORIOUS BRANCH

Dearest Jesus, how will I ever be able to admire you enough, much less adore you, for the wonderful way you stooped to our level?

What an image you used in the vine to illustrate your lowliness and meekness! It reminds us also of your fruitfulness and love for your people.

The prophecy said you would be "like a root out of dry ground." What is more dry and unpromising, before the budding season, than the vine?

It was also said that you would have "no form nor comeliness … no beauty that we should desire" you. And when you call yourself "the true vine," Lord, you could not have chosen a more unsightly image.

It was said that you would be lowly and meek when coming with salvation. And what is lower than the vine, that sends forth branches upon the ground? What is so weak and feeble as the vine, that always needs some prop to support her feeble arms?

In the spreading of your gospel, Lord, your reach was prophesied to be "from sea to sea, and from the River to the ends of the earth." And truly, Lord, in the wide-spreading branches of the vine, you are the fruitful bough of Joseph, "a fruitful bough by a fountain; his branches run over the wall."

So when we see the multitude of your people all hanging on you, all united to you, and all drawing sap, moisture, life, strength, and fruitfulness from you, what can more beautifully represent you and your people than the rich vine and her branches?

Precious Lord Jesus, surely you are the true vine which surpasses the whole creation of God. Lord, let me sit under your shadow, and let me taste of your fruit.

Glorious, wonderful Man, whose name is the Branch! You are as the prophet described you: beautiful and glorious in the eyes of all your redeemed.

On you, Lord, I would hang all the glory of your Father's house, and all the glory of my salvation.

Let me sit under your shadow with great delight here, until you bring me home to sit under you, the tree of life, in the paradise of God, in the fullness of enjoyment of you forever, amen.

— *Robert Hawker*

YOU ARE THE LIGHT!

Precious Jesus, you are the Source, the Fountain, the Author, the Finisher of all.

"O the depth of the riches both of the wisdom and the knowledge of God! How unsearchable are your judgments, and your ways past tracing out!"

What was the day, the ever-blessed, ever-to-be-remembered day, when you—who commanded the light to shine out of darkness—shone in upon my heart?

And when did Jesus, the day-dawn and the day-star, arise to give us "the light of the knowledge of the glory of God in the face of Jesus Christ"?

Glorious light and life of my soul! Continue your sweet influence, morning by morning, at dawn, and during the evening star of your grace. Continue until, after many wintry days of my blindness, ignorance, and senseless state, you renew me in the precious discoveries of your love.

By this I am carried through all the twilight of this poor dying state of things below. For then I will awake to the full enjoyment of you in glory. I will see you in one full, open day; and I will be made like you in your kingdom of light, and life, and happiness, forever and ever. Amen.

— *Robert Hawker*

THE LORD WILL COME INTO HIS GARDEN

Precious Jesus, revive your feeble people, and pour water upon him that is thirsty, and floods upon the dry ground.

In you, blessed Lord, there is fullness to supply all. Surely you are a fountain of gardens, a well of living waters, and streams from Lebanon.

Oh Lord, send forth today abundant streams to cleanse, revive, comfort, satisfy, and strengthen all your churches. Lord, cause me to drink of the rivers of your pleasure, for you are the fountain of life.

All the pleasant and precious fruits of the Spirit are laid at the gates of worship and the word of your gospel. They come anew and in fresh supply from you, sweet and refreshing. By faith, and in your leading and strength, you enable me to bring them home, to live upon them, and feed upon them from day to day! You lay them up in my heart.

And will I not then, blessed Jesus, by the endearing name of my beloved, call upon you to command the north wind and the south wind to blow upon your garden in my heart and in my soul?

Then the spices will flow, and my beloved will come into his garden, and eat of his own pleasant fruits which his grace alone planted, and which his Spirit brings forth and ripens. Amen.

— *Robert Hawker*

THE HEAVENS DECLARE YOUR GLORY

The heavens declare your glory, O God, and the firmament shows your handiwork. And by the things that are made, we clearly see and understand your eternal power and divine nature.

So anyone who says there is no God is a fool without excuse. Truly there is a reward for the righteous, and truly there is a God that judges on the earth, and in heaven too. We therefore come to you, believing that you are, and that you are the powerful and bountiful one.

Who is a God like you, glorious in holiness, fearful in praises, doing wonders? Who in the heavens can be compared to you?

O Lord of Hosts, who is a strong Lord like you? Among the gods there is none like you, O Lord. And there are no works like your works. For you are great, and do wondrous things. You are God alone. No creature has an arm like God, or can thunder with a voice like you.

You are God, not human. You do not have eyes of flesh, and you do not see things as we do. Your days are not as our days.

As heaven is high above the earth, so are your thoughts above our thoughts, and your ways above our ways. All nations before you are like a drop in the bucket, or a speck of dust on the balance.

You are the King eternal, immortal, invisible. Before the mountains were brought forth, or you had formed the earth and the world, from everlasting to everlasting, you are God—the same yesterday, today, and forever.

From of old you laid the foundation of the earth, and the heavens are the work of your hands. The created things will perish, but you will endure. All of them will wear out like a garment, but you are the same, and your years will have no end.

You are God, and you do not change. Therefore we are not consumed. Are you not from everlasting, O Lord our God, our Holy One? The everlasting God, the Lord, the Creator of the ends of the earth, who does not faint or grow weary—there is no searching your understanding. Amen.

— *Matthew Henry*

ALL IS IN YOUR HAND

Your understanding, Lord, is infinite. You number the stars, and call them by name.

You are wonderful in counsel, and excellent in your work. Wise in heart, and mighty in strength.

O Lord, you have done so many works in wisdom, you have done them all by the counsel of your own will. Your wisdom and knowledge are deep! Your judgments unsearchable! Your ways beyond finding out!

The heavens are yours, and all the hosts of them. The earth is yours, and its fullness. The world, and all that live here.

In your hand are the deep places of the earth, and the strength of the hills is yours. The sea is yours, for you made it, and your hands formed the dry land.

All the forest animals are yours, and the cattle on a thousand hills.

You are a great God and King, above all gods.

In your hand is the soul of every living thing, and the breath of all mankind. Your dominion is everlasting, and your kingdom from generation to generation. You do according to your will in the armies of heaven, and among the inhabitants of the earth. No one can stop you or question you.

We know, O God, that you can do everything, and that no thought can be withheld from you. Power belongs to you, and with you nothing is impossible.

All power is yours, in heaven and earth. You kill and you make alive. You wound and you heal. No one can be delivered out of your hand. What you have promised, you are able also to do. Amen.

— Matthew Henry

JESUS THE DOORKEEPER

Lord Jesus, you were a doorkeeper to your own house, that in all things you might be first!

You, like the Jewish servant, submitted to having your ear bored at the doorpost, to go out no more free, but to remain forever. And it was all because of the love you had for your Master, and for your church—your wife and your children.

As I think on the kind of love that is beyond understanding, give me grace to cry out, "I would rather be a doorkeeper in the house of my God than to dwell in the tents of wickedness." Amen.

— Robert Hawker

YOU ARE HOLY

You are holy, you that inhabit the praises of Israel.

Your name is holy and revered, and we give thanks when we remember your holiness.

Your pure eyes will not behold sin. Evil will not dwell with you. You are the rock, your work is perfect, and all your ways are truth and judgment. You are a God of truth, in whom there is no iniquity.

You are our rock, and there is no unrighteousness in you. You are holy in all your works, and holiness becomes your house, O Lord, forever.

You are righteous, O God, when we plead with you. You will be justified when you speak, and clear when you judge.

Your righteousness is like the great mountains, and your judgments are a great deep. Though clouds and darkness are round about you, yet judgment and justice are the habitation of your throne.

You are good, and your mercy endures forever. Your lovingkindness is great toward us, and your truth endures to all generations.

You have proclaimed your name: the Lord God, merciful and gracious, slow to anger, abundant in goodness and truth. You show mercy for thousands. You forgive iniquity, transgression, and sin.

And your name is our strong tower. You are good, and do good—good to all; and your tender mercy is over all your works.

You are good to Israel in a special way, to those with clean hearts. Cause your goodness to pass before us, that we may taste and see that you are good, and always see your lovingkindness. Amen.

— Matthew Henry

You have made me, Lord

Precious Lord Jesus, you have done everything for me, and brought about everything in me.

You formed me from the womb, and now you have made me in yourself.

You have redeemed me, and washed me from my sins in your blood. You bore with me in all my unworthiness, and carried me in all my sorrows!

Into your gracious hands, Lord, I desire to fall this night, and every night, and in the night of death—under the blessed assurance that when my heart faints, and my strength fails, you will be the strength of my heart, and my portion forever. Amen.

— Robert Hawker

YOU ARE ON YOUR THRONE

How small a part of you do we see, God? Only a partial picture.

Who can understand the thunder of your power? Touching the Almighty, we cannot comprehend you. You are excellent in power, judgment, and justice. You are exalted far above all blessing and praise.

You have prepared your throne of glory in the heavens, high and lifted up. Before you the seraphim cover their faces.

And in compassion to us you hold back the face of that throne, spreading a cloud upon it.

You make your angels spirits, and your ministers a flame of fire. Thousands of them minister to you, and ten thousand times ten thousand stand before you, to do what you ask. They excel in strength, and obey your word.

And we come by faith, hope, and holy love into spiritual communion with that innumerable company of angels, and the spirits of just people made perfect. We come to the general assembly and church of the firstborn, in the heavenly Jerusalem.

You are worthy, O Lord, to receive blessing, and honor, and glory, and power. For you have created all things. You created them to do your will and to praise you.

We worship the one who made heaven and earth, the sea and the fountains of waters. The one who spoke and it was done. Who commanded, and it stood fast. The one who said, "Let there be light," and there was light.

And you made it all very good, and it continues this day according to your word, for everything serves you.

The day is yours, the night also is yours. You have prepared the light and the sun. You have set all the borders of the earth. You have made summer and winter. You uphold all things by the word of your power, and by you all things exist.

The earth is full of your riches; so is the great and wide sea. The eyes of all wait upon you, and you give them their food in due season. You open your hand and satisfy the needs of every living thing. Amen.

— *Matthew Henry*

YOU ARE THE POTTER

You are God our Maker. You teach us more than the
animals, and make us wiser than the birds.

We are the clay, and you our potter; we are the work of
your hand.

You took us out of the womb, and kept us safe when we
were infants. We have depended on you from the womb,
and have been held up by you.

You are our God since we were inside our mother, and so
we will never stop praising you. In you, O God, we live,
and move, and have our being. We are your offspring. Our
breath is in your hand, and you are all our ways.

For the way of humanity is not in ourselves. We do not
direct our own steps; our time is in your hand.

You are the God who has fed us all our lives until this day,
and redeemed us from all evil.

It is only by your mercy that we are not consumed,
because your compassions never fail. They are new every
morning; great is your faithfulness.

If you take away our breath, we die, and return to the dust
out of which we were taken.

Who can say a thing, and make it happen, if you do not
command it? Amen.

— *Matthew Henry*

YOU KNIT US TOGETHER

You alone are the Lord.

You have made heaven, the heaven of heavens, with all their host. You made the earth, and all things that are in it. You made the sea, and all that is in it—and you preserve them all.

The host of heaven worship you, whose kingdom rules over all.

A sparrow does not fall to the ground without you knowing. You made man at first from the dust of the ground, and breathed into him the breath of life, so that he became a living soul. And you have made of one blood all nations of people to dwell on the earth. You have determined the boundaries of our lives.

You are the Most High, who rules our kingdoms, and gives them to whoever you decide. You judge us all.

Hallelujah, the Lord God omnipotent reigns. You do all things according to the counsel of your own will, to the praise of your own glory.

We pay our respect to the Father, the Word, and the Holy Spirit, for these three are one.

We adore you, Father, Lord of heaven and earth. And we adore you, eternal Word, who was in the beginning with God, and was God. All things were made by you. Nothing was made without you.

At just the right time you were made flesh, lived among us, and showed your glory—the only begotten of the Father, full of grace and truth.

And since it is God's will that everyone should honor the Son as they honor the Father, we adore you as the brightness of the Father's glory, the exact image of his person.

We join the angels to worship you. We pay our respect to the exalted Redeemer, who is the faithful witness, the first begotten from the dead, and the Prince of the kings of the earth.

We confess that Jesus Christ is Lord, to the glory of God the Father.

We also worship the Holy Spirit, the Comforter, whom the Son has sent from the Father. He is the Spirit of truth, who proceeds from the Father, and who is sent to teach us all things, and bring all things to our remembrance, who composed the Scriptures, holy men of God writing them as they were moved by the Holy Spirit.

You, O God, made us, and not we ourselves. So we are not our own, but yours. We are your people, and the sheep of your pasture. Therefore we worship, fall down, and kneel before the Lord our Maker.

You, Lord, formed our bodies. They are fearfully and wonderfully made, and intricately formed.

You have clothed us with skin and flesh, you have fenced us with bones and sinews, you have granted us life and favor, and your presence preserves our spirits.

You are the Father of our spirits, for you formed our spirits within us, and made us these souls. The Spirit of God has made us, and the breath of the Almighty has given us life. You put wisdom in the inward parts, and give our hearts understanding. Amen.

— *Matthew Henry*

WE WORSHIP JESUS, GOD AND MAN

Christ Jesus, you are true and eternal God, and true and holy man—all in one. You retain the properties of both natures in the unity of your person.

We acknowledge you, and we worship you. We come to you and fall at your feet. We look for salvation from your hand alone.

You are the only Savior. We desire to be your exclusive property. We are by your grace, and will remain that way forever.

Let the whole world of your elect, with us, know, acknowledge, and adore you, and thus finally be saved by you.

This is the sum total of our faith and hope. This is the height of all our wishes. Amen.

— *Herman Witsius*

TO APPROACH AN INFINITE GOD

O Lord, we know so little of your supreme deity, and cannot comprehend your perfection.

Our thoughts about you, your attributes, and your sovereignty fall far short—you are infinite and immense.

What mortal can even begin to set bounds on your sovereignty, where you do not lead the way? We know you are indebted to no one, and no one can ask you "What are you doing?" or "Why are you doing that?"

You are holy and infinitely good. And you both love and reward holiness.

May we recognize just how ignorant we are, and may that kindle in our hearts a vision to know as we are known, and then to see some of those things in your infinity that we could never reach on our own. Amen.

— *Herman Witsius*

HELP ME BEGIN
the DAY.

A PRAYER FOR THE MORNING

O most mighty and glorious God, full of incomprehensible power and majesty, whose glory the very heaven of heavens is not able to contain!

Look down from heaven upon me, your unworthy servant. I prostrate myself at the footstool of your throne of grace. But look upon me, O Father, through the merits and mediation of Jesus Christ, your beloved Son, in whom only you are well pleased.

Of myself, I am not worthy to stand in your presence, or to speak with my unclean lips to so holy a God as you. For you know that in sin I was conceived and born, and that I have lived ever since in iniquity. I have broken all your holy commandments by sinful motions, unclean thoughts, evil words, and wicked works.

I have neglected many of those duties which you require, and committed vices which you, under the penalty of your displeasure, have forbidden.

O Lord, I do here with a grieving heart confess my secret sins. I stand here guilty of your curse for these sins, with all the miseries of this life, and everlasting torments in hell, if you were to deal with me as I deserved.

I confess that your mercy endures forever, Lord. Your compassion never fails. With you there is mercy and abundant redemption. So in the multitude of your mercy, and in confidence in Christ's merit, I beg your divine Majesty that you would not enter into judgment with me.

Do not bring my failures to light. If you did, no flesh could be justified in your sight, no living person could stand in your presence.

But be merciful to me, and wash away all the uncleanness of my sin, with the merits of that precious blood which Jesus Christ has shed for me.

And seeing that he has borne the burden of that curse which was due to me for my transgressions, deliver me from my sins and from all those judgments which hang over my head. Separate them as far from your presence as the east is from the west. Bury them in the burial of Christ, that they may never have power to rise up against me, to shame me in this life, or to condemn me in the world to come.

And I beg you, O Lord, not only to wash away my sins with the blood of your flawless Lamb, but also to purge my heart by your Holy Spirit from the filth of my natural corruption. Help me to feel your Spirit more and more killing the power and practice of my sin, so that I may with more freedom of mind and liberty of will serve you in righteousness and holiness.

And give me grace, that by the direction and help of the Holy Spirit, I may persevere to be your faithful and true servant my whole life. So when this mortal life is ended, may I share the immortality and everlasting happiness in your heavenly kingdom. Amen.

— *Lewis Bayly*

MORNING PRAYER AND THANKSGIVING

As you add days to my life, Lord, I beg you to add repentance and correction. As I grow older, may I also increase in grace and favor with you and all your people.

Supply me with the graces that you know I lack and need. Increase the good gifts you have already given me, so I may be an example, leading a godly life and glorifying your name in everything I say.

May my soul more cheerfully feed on the peace that comes from a good conscience, replenished with the joy of the Holy Spirit.

I give you my most humble and heartfelt thanks for all those blessings which by your goodness you have given me. Of your free love, according to your eternal purpose, you have chosen me before the foundation of the world was laid, for salvation in Jesus Christ.

You have created me in your own image, and have begun to restore that in me which was lost in our first parents. You have called me by the working of your Spirit, in the preaching of the gospel, and the receiving of the sacraments, to the knowledge of your saving grace, and obedience to your blessed will.

You have bought and redeemed me with the blood of your only-begotten Son. You have saved me from the torments of hell and the bondage of Satan.

You have freely justified me by faith in Christ, made me right with God—even though I am by nature a child of wrath.

You have sanctified me by your Holy Spirit, made me holy, and given me much time to repent, along with the means of repentance.

Good Lord, I thank you for my life, health, wealth, food, clothing, peace, prosperity, and plenty. Thank you for preserving me this night from all perils and dangers of body and soul, and for bringing me safe to the beginning of this day.

As you have now awakened my body from sleep, so, I beg you, awaken my soul from sin and from worldly security. As you have caused the light of day to shine in my physical eyes, so cause the light of your word and Holy Spirit to illuminate my heart.

Give me grace, as one of your children of light, to walk in holy obedience before your face this day. Help me to keep faith and a clear conscience toward you, and toward all, in all my thoughts, words, and dealings.

And so, good Lord, bless my work today, that I may give you glory and strive for the good of others, adding comfort of my own soul and conscience in that day when I will make my final account to you. Amen.

— *Lewis Bayly*

MORNING PLEADING FOR BLESSINGS

Keep your servant, O God, that I may do no evil to anyone this day. Let it be your blessed will not to allow the devil nor his wicked angels, nor any of his evil members, or my enemies, to have any power to do me hurt or violence.

Watch over me for good and not for evil, and command your holy angels to pitch their tents around me, for my defense and safety in my going out and coming in, as you have promised they should do for those who fear your name.

Into your hands, O Father, I do here commit my soul and body, my actions, and all that I ever have, to be guided, defended, and protected by you.

I am assured that whatever you take into your custody cannot perish, nor suffer any hurt or harm. And if I at any time this day will through frailty forget you, even so Lord, I beg you, in mercy—remember me.

And I pray not for myself alone, but I beg you also to be merciful to your whole church, your chosen people, wherever they live upon the earth. Defend them from the rage and tyranny of the devil, the world, and the antichrist.

Give your gospel a free and a joyful passage through the world, for the conversion of those you have chosen. Bless the churches and countries we live in with the peace, justice, and true faith.

Bless our country's leaders, and increase in them the gifts and spiritual graces which make them fit for those jobs where you have placed them. Direct the leaders of our country and our churches to lead the people in true faith, justice, obedience, and peace.

Be merciful to the believers who fear you and call upon your name. And comfort as many among them as are sick and comfortless in body or mind. Especially be favorable to all who suffer any trouble or persecution for the testimony of your truth and your holy gospel. In your grace, deliver them out of all their troubles—however is best in your wisdom, for the glory of your name, for the further expansion of the truth, and for the increase of their own comfort and consolation.

Hasten your coming, blessed Savior, and end these sinful days. Give me grace, that like a wise virgin I may be prepared with oil in my lamp to meet you, the blessed bridegroom, at your coming. Whether it be by my day of death, or at the day of judgment, Lord Jesus, come when you will; come quickly!

These, and all other graces which you know I need, this day and evermore, I humbly beg and crave at your hands, O Father. I give you the glory, amen.

— *Lewis Bayly*

ANOTHER MORNING PRAYER

Thank you for defending me this night from all perils and dangers, Lord, and for bringing me safe to the beginning of this day. Keep me today from all evil that may hurt me, and from falling into any sin that should offend you.

From the bottom of my heart, Lord, I thank you for all your blessings you have bestowed on my soul and body. For choosing me in your love, for redeeming me by your Son, for sanctifying me by your Spirit, and for preserving me until this present day and hour by your gracious providence.

Set your fear before my eyes, and let your Spirit rule my heart, so that all I think, do, or speak this day may lead to your glory, the good of others, and the peace of my own conscience.

I commit myself, and all my ways and actions, together with all that belong to me, to your gracious direction and protection. Keep both them and me from all evil, and bless our honest labors and endeavors.

Send your Holy Spirit into my heart to assure me that you are my Father, that I am your child, and that you love me with an unchangeable love. And let the same good Spirit lead me in your truth, and crucify in me more and more all worldly lusts, that my sins may more and more die in me, and that I may serve you in sincere righteousness and holiness this day and all the days of my life. And when this life is ended, through your mercy in Christ, let me share in your everlasting glory in your heavenly kingdom.

Defend your whole church. Preserve our country's
leaders. Bless our pastors. Comfort those who are sick
and comfortless. And keep me ready, Lord, by faith
and repentance, for my last day. May I be found in
you, whether I live or die, to your eternal glory and my
everlasting salvation, through Jesus Christ my only Savior,
in whose blessed name I beg these mercies at your hands,
and give to you your praise and glory, amen.

— *Lewis Bayly*

A PRAYER AS WE AWAKE

O Lord our God and Heavenly Father! We, your
unworthy children, come into your most holy and
heavenly presence to give you praise and glory for your
great mercies and blessings—especially that you have
preserved us this night past and have given us quiet rest to
our bodies, and brought us now safely to the beginning of
this day.

Lord, open our eyes every day more and more to see and
consider your great and marvelous love to us, that our
hearts may be drawn yet nearer to you—even more to love
you, fear you, and obey you.

Compel us to come into your most glorious presence with
new songs of thanksgiving in our mouths.

Nail down all our sins and iniquities to the cross of
Christ, bury them in his death, bathe them in his blood,
hide them in his wounds, and let them never rise up in
judgment against us.

Good Father, touch our heart with true repentance for all sin. Let us not take any pleasure in any sin, but however we fall through frailty, as we fall often, yet never let us fall finally. Let us never lie down in sin, nor continue in sin, but let us get upon our feet again, turn to you with all our heart, and seek you while you may be found, and while you extend grace and mercy to us.

Lord, increase in us that true faith that allows us to lay sure hold on your Son, and rest on his merits.

Give us the faith to believe all the great and precious promises made in the gospel. Strengthen us from above to walk in all the true and sound fruits of faith. Let us not walk in the flesh, but in the Spirit.

Let us feel the power of your Son's death killing sin in our mortal bodies, and the power of his resurrection raising us up to newness of life.

Let us grow daily in the sanctification of the Spirit, and the death of the flesh. Let us live holy, just, and sober lives, shining as lights in this present evil world. Fill us with your Spirit. Stir us to prayer and watchfulness, reading and meditating on your law.

Have mercy on us, and never leave us to ourselves, nor to our own wills, lusts, or desires. Help us with your good Spirit, that we may continue to the end, be received into glory, and partake of that immortal crown you have laid up for all who love you. Amen.

— Arthur Dent

PRAYERS THROUGHOUT THE DAY

Lord, we always depend on your grace and hand in our lives.
When I am about to pray, Lord, fix my attention! Awaken
my holy affections, and pour out upon me the spirit of grace
and of supplication (Zechariah 12:10).

When I open my Bible—or any other good book—open
my eyes, that I may behold wondrous things out of your
law (Psalm 119:18). Enlighten my understanding and warm
my heart. Confirm my best intentions and keep me on the
right path in life.

When it is time to focus on business, Lord, grant your
favor, and establish the work of our hands (Psalm 90:17).
Give your blessing to my honest endeavors.

When it is time for recreation, Lord, bless my refreshments.
Let me not forget you in them, but still keep your glory
in view.

When I meet with others, Lord, may no corrupting talk
come from my mouth, but only what is good for building
up, as fits the occasion, that it may give grace to those who
hear (Ephesians 4:29).

When I face difficulties, Lord, give me the wisdom which
gives success (Ecclesiastes 10:10). Teach me your way, and
lead me in a clear path (Psalm 27:11).

When I encounter temptations, let your strength, O
gracious Redeemer, be made perfect in my weakness
(2 Corinthians 12:9). Amen.

— Philip Doddridge

PRESERVE ME THROUGH THIS DAY

Lord God, you know I need to call on you for my daily bread. But how much more reason I have to crave the graces of your Holy Spirit—for supplying my soul with heavenly food, and especially with saving faith.

When I am tossed about with the storms of doubts and fears, show me how to lay hold of your word and promises. Then all the temptations of the world, the flesh, and the devil will never prevail over me, since I know in whom I have believed.

Increase the light of my faith, that it may daily cast forth more clear beams. Preserve that faith in the darkness of death, that it may guide me to eternal life.

And rule and govern me by your Holy Spirit, that I may never lose faith by agreeing to do anything that is against the light of my conscience.

Confirm the good work you have begun in me, strengthen me inwardly, and preserve me blameless until the day of the Lord Jesus Christ, that I may inherit eternal life. Amen.

— *Robert Parker*

MORNING PRAYER

Come, Lord. I pray that your sweet influences would fill
my mouth with your words, and that you would warm my
heart with your love. Bring me to your mercy seat today,
this morning, as you loose my tongue and enlarge my
heart with your grace.

Yes, blessed Jesus, you will hear my voice in the morning. I
will direct my prayers to you at the dawn of the day. I will
send them up to heaven, and through the day, and all the
day, and seven times a day. I will praise you, God of my
salvation, when you cause me to praise you with joyful
lips.

Precious Spirit of all truth, glorify the Lord Jesus. Show
me the things of Christ, and grant me daily fellowship
and communion with the Father, and with his Son Jesus
Christ!

Let the sense of your freeness in salvation comfort my
soul. Help me understand that there was no yoke upon
you, Lord, except your own everlasting love. Be the sweet
constraining yoke on my soul, to bind me to your love and
to your service forever.

Be ever with me, Lord. And as Jesus promised, abide with
me forever. May I never grieve you by whom my soul is
sealed in Jesus to the day of eternal redemption.

— *Robert Hawker*

HELP ME LIVE THE DAY.

Fighting the Daily Fight

Dear God, it is so hard for us to fight against ourselves.

It is very difficult to overcome an enemy that lies so close and hidden within us as our flesh does. And unless you arm me with divine power, I am in great danger of yielding to this treacherous foe.

Help me die to myself daily, I beg you. Do not let me be eternally separated by the attractions of the flesh from the life that is in Christ my Savior.

Preserve me this day in your fear and favor, and in the end bring me to your everlasting kingdom, through Jesus Christ. Amen.

— *Robert Parker*

Preserve us, God

Through Christ, the only master and teacher of his church, to you be praise forever.

God the Father, for your Son Christ's sake, show your mercy every time we stray. Reveal our sins to us more and more. Keep us in, and lead us to your truth.

Show us how to be faithful in everything we have received, whether it be less or more, and preserve us against all the scandals the whole world is filled with. Amen.

— *John Robinson*

WHERE COULD WE EVER HIDE FROM YOU?

No one can hide in secret places that you cannot see, for you fill heaven and earth. You are not far from every one of us. We cannot go anywhere that is beyond your presence, nor flee from your Spirit.

If we ascend into heaven, you are there. If we make our bed in hell, in the depths of the earth, you are there. If we take the wings of the morning, or live in the uttermost parts of the sea, even there your hand will lead us, and your right hand will hold us.

We cannot outrun you.

All things are naked and open before your eyes—even the thoughts and intents of the heart.

Your eyes are in every place, beholding good and evil. You see everywhere, proving yourself strong on behalf of those whose hearts are right with you. You search the heart, that you may give to everyone according to their ways, and according to the fruit of their lives.

O God, you have searched us and known us. You know when we sit down and when we get up. You understand our thoughts from afar. You surround our path and our lying-down, and you know all our ways. You know every word we speak. Darkness and light are both alike to you.

Such knowledge is too wonderful for us. Amen.

— *Matthew Henry*

A PRAYER OF EVERYDAY GRATITUDE

What can I say but this, Lord: my heart admires you, and adores you, and loves you.

My little vessel is as full as it can hold, and I would pour out all that fullness before you to receive more and more.

You are my hope and my help, my glory, and the lifter-up of my head (Psalm 3:3). My heart rejoices in your salvation (Psalm 13:5).

And when your Spirit allows me to converse with you, a thousand wonderful thoughts flow into my soul with refreshment and joy. They seem to crowd the happiness of many months into every single moment.

In humble wonder, I bless you for the knowledge and grace that lifts and sanctifies my soul—though it does not flourish as much as I could wish.

I bless you also for the body you have given me, the senses I enjoy. And even more importantly, I bless you for the strength and ability to serve you.

I bless you for the ability to move—under my own power, and guided by yours. Your hand stays close, strengthening my nerves and restoring my strength.

I praise you for the bounty you provide every day for all people, for the tables you spread before me, and for the overflowing cup you place in my hands. I do not take this bounty for granted, as I share it with so many good friends.

Thank you for so many dear relatives at home, and for kind friends abroad. Thank you that they can help me when needed, and that you also enable me to serve them, since it is "more blessed to give than to receive" (Acts 20:35).

Thank you for a heart that feels the sorrows of those in need, and a mind that can think of ways to serve—even with my small ability. This comes from you, Lord. You are the author of every caring act, every wise plan, and every successful attempt to spread happiness or relieve pain.

Thank you for granting me compassion for those in need, as well as for those already blessed.

I adore you for the streams that water paradise, maintaining it in ever-flourishing, ever-growing delight. I praise you for the rest and overwhelming joy you are giving to many who were once dear to me on earth. My job was to ease their pain and promote their joy.

Thank you for the blessing of every saint and angel that surrounds your throne. I praise you for the hope you planted in my heart: that I will soon experience firsthand what I now see only dimly, from a distance.

Even now, through your grace, I feel your supporting arm leading me toward heaven. I await your salvation with a blend of that passionate desire believers cannot help feeling, and a calm surrender born of your unchanging promise. Amen.

— *Philip Doddridge*

WHEN GOD VISITS MY TABLE

Yes, dearest Jesus! I am truly yours, by every tie which can make me yours. I am yours by the gift of God the Father, by your marriage contract with me, by the Holy Spirit anointing me in you, making me one with you—and in you—before the world.

Yes, generous Lord! I come to buy from you with no money in hand—because I know very well, through your teaching, that neither the obedience of people or of angels can purchase any connection to you. It is only through your own precious merits and your atoning blood.

So now, Lord, possessing you, I possess all things. I will give up everything else, and forget about everything else, since Jesus is mine, and I am his, in time and to all eternity.

Precious, precious Jesus! I bless your name that I hear your voice. Your loud and powerful knocks, by your word and by your Spirit, have made me eager for you to come in.

Put in your hand, Lord, by the door opening, and open my heart. Give me grace to receive you, to embrace you, to love you, to delight in you, to welcome you.

I would say, in the warmth and desire of my soul, and in the language of your own most sacred words: "Lift up your heads, O you gates; and be lifted up, you everlasting doors—and the King of glory will come in!"

And what have you promised, Lord, when the door of my poor heart is opened?

You have said, "I will come in to him, and will dine with him, and he with me."

Bountiful Lord! Will you really give me the precious privilege of a union with you? Communion with you and your graces? Will you feed and feast me at my poor house?

I have nothing to set before you; I can offer nothing good enough for you to accept. But I hear you say, "I am the bread of life, and the bread of God that comes down from heaven." I am all, and provide all!

Lord, I fall down under a deep sense of my vileness and your glory, my emptiness and your all-sufficiency.

Blessed Master! Be my all in all, and let my poor soul feast on your fullness. Amen.

— *Robert Hawker*

TO THE HOLY SPIRIT

Holy Spirit, finish the healing, saving work of Jesus my Lord, and do not let the flesh or the world prevail.

Let not my nights be so long and my days so short, nor sin eclipse those beams which have often illuminated my soul.

Without you, books are senseless scrawls, studies are dreams, and knowledge is foolishness.

Be in me the resident witness of my Lord, the author of my prayers, the Spirit of adoption, the seal of God, and the deposit of my inheritance.

Transcribe those sacred words on my heart that by your inspiration are recorded in your holy word. Bring that love upon my heart that may keep it in a continual life of love.

Teach me the work which I must do in heaven, refresh my soul with the delights of holiness, and show me the joys which arise from the believing hopes of the everlasting joys.

Exercise my heart and tongue in the holy praises of my Lord. Strengthen me in sufferings, and conquer the terrors of death and hell.

Make me more heavenly. And let my last thoughts, words,
and works on earth be like those which will be my first
in the place of glorious immortality—the place where
the kingdom is delivered up to the Father, and God will
forever be all, and in all.

And the Lord of whom and through whom and to whom
are all things—to him be glory forever. Amen.

— *Richard Baxter*

What kind of Christians are we?

"You do not need me to write to you about brotherly love,"
says the apostle Paul, "for you yourselves are taught by
God to love one another" (1 Thessalonians 4:9).

Lord, that one text is enough by itself to pierce our hearts
through and through.

Lord, are we the same kind of Christians today as they
were then? I pray that it would be that way with us, that
we would not need to be written to, or preached to,
concerning this.

Is it obvious by the way we treat each other, that you
yourself have taught us to love one another? Amen.

— *Jeremiah Burroughs*

A MIDDAY PRAYER FOR PERSPECTIVE

Show me how to love the word, that my bold love for you would increase.

Remind me that the fashions of the world pass away, and their momentary glory will vanish into emptiness and nothing.

Draw my heart to you and set my mind on things that will last forever.

Help me love you fiercely, and cleave to you with a perfect heart. May nothing here satisfy my soul.

Protect me through the rest of this day, that I may fall into no temptation, and no danger of soul or body, for the sake of Jesus Christ my blessed Redeemer. Amen.

— *Robert Parker*

THANKS BEFORE A MEAL

Most gracious God and loving Father, you feed all living creatures, and they depend on your divine providence. Now we ask that you would set apart those that you have ordained for us, make them able to nourish our bodies in life and health. And give us grace to receive them with thanks, remembering that they are from your hand. In the strength of these and your other blessings, help us to walk before you today and all the days of our lives in a way that is pleasing to you, through our Lord and only Savior Jesus Christ. Amen.

— *Lewis Bayly*

HELP ME CLOSE
THE DAY.

A PRAYER BEFORE I DIE

Dearest Jesus, I pray for more of that grace, for more of that faith, to overcome all fears, doubts, and misgivings.

If only you would show me, dear Lord, day by day, that the nearer I draw to the time of my death, the closer I may cling to your embraces, and the more I may hang my soul upon you.

When death comes, may you give such strength to my poor dying body, that like the patriarch I may cry out, "Into your hand I commend my spirit. You have redeemed me, O Lord, God of truth!"

Precious Jesus, you are the fairest and the first among ten thousand. I pray, Lord: be to me like the fruitful branch which the dying patriarch blessed, whose branches ran over the wall.

You give strength to my poor feeble faith, to gather all the rich fruits of your righteousness for the healing of my soul, so every day I can sit down under your shadow with great delight. Your fruit is sweet to my taste.

Lord the Spirit! I ask you, glorify my Redeemer in my poor cold and lifeless heart. Lead my affections to my all-precious Jesus, that I may live with him, and feel my claim in his great salvation grow stronger and more precious.

Holy Lord! Keep alive, I beg you, your saving and powerful presence in my heart, that I may never, never by sin, put out your divine flame, nor grieve the Holy Spirit, who seals me for the day of redemption.

Precious Redeemer, dying Lamb of God, were my sins adding to your sorrow? Have I looked down on unbelievers, and all the while forgetting that every sin of mine became more painful to your soul than the cross, or the thorns, or the soldier's spear that pierced your heart?

Oh! For grace to crucify those sins which nailed you to the cursed tree! Oh! For grace to take up the cross and follow you, day by day. Lord Jesus, give me grace to go forth to you.

Precious, precious Redeemer! I pray for a full tide of your grace to be poured in upon my soul when it is time to set my house in order, since you were pleased to awaken me to the knowledge of you and a desire for you.

In the end, may I finally, fully, and completely—once for all—cast my soul into your blessed arms, as I say "Lord Jesus, receive my spirit." Amen.

— *Robert Hawker*

PRAYER OF REPENTANCE FOR THE EVENING

O most gracious God and loving Father, you know my lying down and my rising up, and you are near to all who call upon you in truth and sincerity. So I implore you to look upon me with the eyes of your mercy—not as unclean or ashamed to lift up my eyes to heaven.

I have grievously sinned against heaven and before you, O Lord. I have transgressed all your commandments, not only through negligence, but often through willful presumption—contrary to the motions of your Holy Spirit reclaiming me from them.

So I have wounded my conscience and grieved your Holy Spirit, by whom you have sealed me to the day of redemption. You have consecrated my soul and body to be the temple of the Holy Spirit; I have defiled both.

My eyes, in taking pleasure to behold vanity.

My ears, in listening to impure speech.

My tongue, in speaking evil.

My hands, so full of impurity that I am ashamed to lift them up to you.

My feet, that carried me in my own directions.

My understanding and reasoning, so quick in all earthly matters, but so blind and stupid when I come to meditate or talk about spiritual and heavenly things.

My memory, which should be the treasury of all goodness, yet is not so apt to remember anything except vile and vain things.

My sins have grown over me like a loathsome skin disease, infecting me from head to toe.

But seeing that by your infinite mercy you have spared me so long, and still wait for my repentance, I humbly implore you, for the sake of the bitter death and passion which Jesus Christ suffered for me, that you would pardon and forgive me all my offences, and open to me that ever-streaming fountain of the blood of Christ, which you have promised to open under the New Testament to those who repent.

I pray that all my sins and uncleanness may be so bathed in his blood, buried in his death, and hid in his wounds, that they may never more be seen, to shame me in this life, or to condemn me before your judgment seat in the world to come.

Amen.

— Lewis Bayly

REFRESH ME TONIGHT, LORD

Set apart to me this night's rest, Lord, that I may enjoy
your sweet blessing and benefit.

With this refreshing sleep, enable me to walk before you,
doing the good works you have appointed. And while I
sleep, you who are the keeper of Israel, you who neither
slumber nor sleep, watch over me in your holy providence.

Protect me from all dangers, so that neither the evil angels
of Satan nor any wicked enemy may have any power to do
me harm. Let your holy angels pitch their tents around me,
for my defense and safety.

Knowing that your name is a strong tower of defense to all
who trust you, I commit myself and all that belong to me
to your holy protection and custody.

And if it is your will to call for me in my sleep, Lord, have
mercy upon me, and receive my soul into your heavenly
kingdom.

But if you are pleased to add more days to my life, make
those days even better than before. Wean my mind from
the love of the world and worldly vanities, and cause me
more and more to talk about heaven and heavenly things.

Perfect in me every day that good work which you have
begun, to the glory of your name and the salvation of my
sinful soul. Amen.

— *Lewis Bayly*

AN EVENING PRAYER

O eternal God and most gracious Father, we your
unworthy servants do cast ourselves at the footstool of
your grace. By nature, nothing good dwells in us. Our
hearts are full of secret pride, anger, impatience, pretending,
lying, lust, vanity, profaneness, and distrust. We love
ourselves and this world too much, and we love you and
your kingdom too little.

For the sake of Jesus Christ your dear Son, have mercy on
us. Pardon and forgive us all our sins, and free us from the
shame and ruin which are due us for them.

And because you have created us to serve you, inspire
your Holy Spirit into our hearts. May we not be blinded in
our sins, but let us more and more come to loathe them.

Let us feel the power of Christ's death killing sin in our
mortal bodies, and the virtue of his resurrection raising up
our souls to newness of life.

Convert our hearts, subdue our affections, regenerate our
minds, and purify our nature.

Increase our faith in the sweet promises of the gospel, and
our repentance from dead works. Increase in us a love
for your children—especially those in need of help and
comfort.

And so by the fruits of piety and a righteous life, may we
be assured that your Holy Spirit dwells in us, and that we
are your children by grace and adoption.

You have been so merciful to us in things of this life, but infinitely more merciful in the things of a better life. We thank you for all your blessings and benefits. You are that Father of lights from whom we have received all good and perfect gifts. To you alone belong all glory, honor, and praise—both now and evermore.

Father, you who never slumbers nor sleeps, would you watch over your children while we sleep? Command your angels to pitch their tents around our home, to guard us from all dangers. As we sleep in you, may we tomorrow morning be awakened by you. And so refreshed, may we be more ready to serve.

Your grace, O Lord Jesus Christ; your love, O Heavenly Father; your comfort and consolation, O holy and blessed Spirit, be with us, and remain with us, this night and evermore. Amen.

— Lewis Bayly

PRAYER OF THANKS FOR THE EVENING

Let your Spirit open my eyes more and more to see the wondrous things of your law, Lord.

Open my lips, that my mouth may daily defend your truth and proclaim your praise.

Increase in me those good gifts which of your mercy you have already given me. And give me a patient spirit, a pure heart and affections, a contented mind, wise behavior. Grant me all those other graces which I need to govern my heart in your fear and guide my life in your favor.

Whether I live or die, may I live and die to you, my God and my Redeemer.

And here, O Lord, I render to you from the altar of my humble heart all possible thanks for those blessings and benefits which you have bestowed upon my soul and body—for this life, and for that which is to come.

Thank you for creating and choosing me. Thank you for redeeming me and putting me to work. Thank you for justifying me and sanctifying me. Thank you for protecting me, from my childhood until now, and for giving me a hope for the future.

Thank you for blessing me with health and resources: food, clothing, and prosperity. And thank you especially for defending me today from perils and dangers of body and soul, and for furnishing me with all the good things I need.

Amen.

— *Lewis Bayly*

An evening prayer of confession

Holy and eternal Lord, I confess those many weaknesses and imperfections which I have been guilty of today. I call on you for the pardon and forgiveness of my sins.

I have heard your word, but with such deadness and distraction, that I have been a very unprofitable and forgetful hearer. I have done your work, but negligently.

But you are rich in mercy and redemption. Do not count against me what I have done wrong. Pardon my transgressions, negligence, and ignorance.

Cover my imperfections with the perfect and absolute obedience of your dear Son. Accept those sacrifices which I have offered to you today in and for that sacrifice Christ Jesus offered upon the cross.

Ease me of the burden of all my sins, and give me grace to arise from the slumber of sin to newness of life. Help me walk according to your holy word, until I attain the end of my faith, the salvation of my soul in the day of the Lord Jesus Christ. Amen.

— *Robert Parker*

ANOTHER EVENING PRAYER

Come, gracious Lord, sit down with me after all the toils of the day. Close the evening with some blessed token of your favor.

I remember your past kindness, and so I feel encouraged to seek a renewal of your love. Dear Lord, do I not know you as a tried, sure, unchanging friend? A brother in adversity?

Knowing you makes me confident about everything that I have now to ask.

Should I go to you, Lamb of God, who died for me, with doubts and fears that you will not claim me or even notice who was bought with your blood?

No! Precious Jesus, I will never dishonor you that way, since you have given me the spirit of adoption, not the spirit of bondage. I will never lose sight of you or this endearing part of your character. Your love, and not what we deserve, is what rules your grace to your people.

Come, then, Lord Jesus, in the stillness of this evening, and show yourself to my heart in ways you do not speak to the world.

Jesus, if you would only speak—even whisper—in the words of your holy Scripture, I would feel all the power, sweetness, and energy of its saving truths.

One view of your heart, Jesus, and the love in it for poor sinners, will drown all the cries of unbelief, all the noise of the world, all the temptations of the enemy.

Then, Lord, for a while, I will forget every sorrow and pain, every difficulty and trial. And then will not the tempter flee, when he sees my poor feeble soul held in the arms of Jesus?

Blessed be my God and Savior! I feel a sense of your strengthening and refreshing presence. My faith lays hold of you, and I will not let you go. You are the hope and Savior of Israel! Amen.

— *Robert Hawker*

AN EVENING PRAYER FOR A CLEAN HEART

Lord, you are my strength and confidence. You are my hope and shield, my defense.

Hear the humble requests I now make at your mercy seat, asking your pardon for all my sins.

Do not give me what I deserve for what I have done. Let your mercy preserve me in holiness and innocence, that I may lead a pure life in truth, humility, and justice.

Plant the good word of truth in my heart, and water it with the dew of your blessed Spirit, that it may always bring forth the fruits of a holy life.

Give me clean hands and a pure heart, Lord. Teach me to follow your example and imitate your holiness, that I may receive from you the eternal rewards and blessings of righteousness.

God of my salvation, let me ascend to where you have gone before. Fill my heart with a longing to enter those courts where you sit among millions of angels and blessed spirits.

Help my heart and eyes to overflow with sorrow and regret for my sins, so I may live a godly life, and may go from strength to strength, until I appear before you and dwell in your courts for all eternity.

And as I pray to you, let me not forget to praise and magnify your name for all your blessings of health, peace, and prosperity, renewed to me every morning.

I give you thanks, eternal Father, for the mercies of this day, and I throw myself on your protection this night from death and danger. If I live another day, may I live in new obedience to all your holy commands, through Jesus Christ. Amen.

— *Robert Parker*

YOUR KINGDOM COME.

THE KINGDOM IS YOURS

Whoever rules in any realm, the kingdom is yours.

They only rule by commission from you, and as substitutes under you. You are the supreme governor of them all. You are exalted as head above all.

Everything is yours, all that is in the heaven and in the earth—yours. Amen.

— *David Clarkson*

A PRAYER FOR THE END TIMES

How melancholy does the face of our earth appear when we reflect on the reign of Satan on it, on the influence of the dragon and the beast and the false prophet.

O Lord, cut short their power. Send down the angel that has the key to the bottomless pit to bind this destroyer. And when he is loosed for a season, moderate his rage and support your saints under the terror of every assault until you appear to close this perplexing scene by the wise and glorious catastrophe of all things.

Then it will be seen that the souls of those who were beheaded for the testimony of Jesus were not lost, and that it was wise to refuse the mark of the beast—though they could neither buy nor sell, nor enjoy their liberty, nor their lives, without submitting to it. Amen.

— *Philip Doddridge*

THE BATTLE BELONGS TO JESUS

How was it, dearest Jesus, that you graciously reached
down to visit your chosen, even so long before your time
on earth? To tell your people that your thoughts were for
good, and not evil?

When you appeared to Joshua in human form as Captain
of the Lord's host, he instantly knew your glorious
character as Mediator, and fell to the earth in adoration.

Hail then, you almighty Lord, you Captain of the Lord's
host, and of my salvation! You have entered the holy war
and led captivity captive. You have fully conquered Satan
and sin, and death, and hell, for your people.

And you will surely conquer all those tremendous foes
of ours, in your people, and bruise Satan under our feet
shortly. Indeed, dear Lord, you have already brought them
under, for by your sovereign grace in the hearts of your
redeemed, you have made your people "willing in the day
of your power."

By the sword of your Spirit, you have convinced my soul of
sin, and by the arrows of your quiver, you have wounded
my heart with deep contrition for sin. Lord, I fall before
you, as your servant Joshua did, and worship you.

And with all the church of the redeemed, both in heaven
and earth, we cheerfully confess "that Jesus Christ is Lord,
to the glory of God the Father." Amen!

— *Robert Hawker*

Even so come, Lord Jesus!

Send forth your convoy of angels for my departing soul, and let them bring it among the perfect spirits of the just. Let me follow my dear friends that have died in Christ before.

And when my friends are crying over my grave, let my spirit be with you in rest.

You who numbers the hairs of my head, number all the days that my body lies in the dust.

Hasten, O my Savior, the time of your return. Send forth your angels, and let that dreadful, joyful trumpet sound.

Do not delay, or the living could give up their hope.

Do not delay, or this earth could grow to be like hell, and your church by divisions be crumbled to dust.

Do not delay, or your enemies could take advantage of your flock. Or pride, hypocrisy, sensuality, and unbelief could prevail against your remnant, and when you came you might not find faith on the earth.

Do not delay, lest the grave should boast of victory.

O hasten that great resurrection day, when your command will go forth, and none will disobey.

That day when the sea and earth yield up their hostages, and all that sleep in the grave awake, and the dead in Christ arise.

That day when the corruptible seed that you sowed comes forth incorruptible.

I entrust myself not to a grave, but to you. My flesh will rest in hope, until you raise it to the everlasting rest.

Return, O Lord! How long? Let your kingdom come! Your desolate bride says *come*, for your Spirit within her says *come*—the one who teaches her to pray with groanings which cannot be expressed.

The whole creation says *come*, waiting to be delivered from the bondage of corruption into the glorious liberty of the children of God.

And you yourself have said, *surely I come.* Amen, even, so come, Lord Jesus.

— *Richard Baxter*

YOUR KINGDOM COME, HERE AND IN HEAVEN

Lead us not into temptation, nor allow us to be assaulted and buffeted by the wicked one. Or if, in your all-wise counsel and purpose, you permit us to be tempted, yet deliver us from the evil to which we are tempted. Let us endure temptations as our affliction, but let us not say yes to them, nor make them our sins.

Thy kingdom come, Lord! Raise, Lord; enlarge, Lord; establish your kingdom! For yours is the glory. And unless you want your glory confined only to heaven, or account the praises and eternal hallelujahs of saints and angels enough adoration for your great name, Lord, have regard to this your poor decaying kingdom.

For only in it, and in heaven, is your glory celebrated.

And if you leave this kingdom to be overrun by the agents and ministers of the devil, or if idolatry and the profane gain ground here so as to push you off the throne, would that not be giving your glory to another—which you have promised not to do?

Lord, you are still the same God. Your essence is eternal. Your attributes will never change. Your power, wisdom, and mercy are the same as ever. So in your mercy, grant us the same favor. Amen.

— *Ezekiel Hopkins*

LOOKING TO REST IN HEAVEN

Forgive, O Lord, the offenses I have committed against
you this day.

I bless your name that you have continued my health and
safety to this evening.

Extend your hand of protection over me this night, that
I may quietly take my rest which you have appointed for
refreshing my weak and weary body.

I ask that when this life ends, and my last sleep comes, that
I may eternally rest with you in your heavenly kingdom.

Grant this, Heavenly Father, for the sake of your Son Jesus
Christ, my only Lord and Savior. Amen.

— Robert Parker

WHAT A MORNING THAT WILL BE

You who are King of nations and King of saints, are also my God and King. For you have a universal empire, being one with the Father over all, blessed forever.

To you I bow the knee, and humbly and gratefully desire to put the crown of my salvation on your head.

And what has this Sovereign done for me? We record your praise; we tell it to saints and sinners everywhere. This great, glorious, condescending King, has not only brought us out of darkness and the shadow of death, but has brought us into his chambers.

What chambers? Chambers of sweet communion and fellowship. Chambers of grace, of love and mercy, of redemption, of ordinances, and of all your covenant blessings.

You have taught me of your love, and my privileges in you, and so assured me of my everlasting safety in you and your finished salvation.

You have assured me that when you have accomplished all your blessed purposes concerning me, you will bring me home into your inner chambers of light and glory. And I will never leave, but dwell in them, and in the presence of God and the Lamb, forever and ever. Hallelujah!

What a morning that will be, different from every other! Lord, how often do I now awake with thoughts of earth, and sin, and trifles, and vanity? How have I opened my eyes this morning? Was it, dearest Jesus, with thoughts of you?

In that solemn morning there will be no longer dreams, as now, even in our waking hours—for all childish fantasies, shadows, doubts, and fears will be done away.

Precious Lord Jesus! Cause me morning by morning, while upon earth, to awaken with sweet thoughts of you. Let the close of night, and the opening of the day, be with your dear name in my heart, on my thoughts, and on my lips.

And in that everlasting morning, after having dropped asleep in Jesus, and in your arms by faith, may I awake in your embraces, and after your likeness, to be everlastingly and eternally satisfied with you. Amen.

— *Robert Hawker*

A PRAYER FOR THE CHURCH

Most loving Father, we humbly ask that you would look down from heaven in great mercy upon your whole church, and every member of it. Be favorable to Zion, and build up the walls of Jerusalem.

Look with an eye of pity on the great ruins and desolation of your church. Heal up the wounds in all the nations. Regard it as your own flock, be gentle as to your own family, care for it as your own vineyard, love it as your own spouse.

Bless it with your grace, guide it with your Spirit, and defend it always with your mighty power.

Scatter, confound, and overthrow any forces that fight against the church, and have mercy on the church in this land. Bless us with true faith.

Deal with us, and with those who come after us, in your grace and favor, for the sake of your great name, and for the sake of our only Mediator Jesus Christ, to whom be all praise and glory, with you and the Holy Spirit, now and forevermore, amen.

— *Arthur Dent*

Notes

1. Leland Ryken, "The Original Puritan Work Ethic," Christian History 89 (2006), https://christianhistoryinstitute.org/magazine/article/original-puritan-work-ethic.

2. Philip Doddridge, "A Prayer for the Success of this Work," in *The Rise and Progress of Religion in the Soul*, 8th ed. (London: Hitch and Hawes, et al., 1761), 11.

3. Joseph Alleine, in the postscript to *An Alarm to Unconverted Sinners* (Hanover, NH: Charles Spear, 1816, first published 1671), 227.

Biographies

Joseph Alleine (1634–1668) faced official persecution during his years of ministry, yet never wavered from his preaching—sometimes traveling with the grandfather of John and Charles Wesley. He was fined and imprisoned several times for refusing to adhere to the Act of Uniformity of 1662, which prescribed officially sanctioned church rites and ceremonies. He and his wife Theodosia worked together tirelessly in neighborhood evangelism and discipleship, and he is best known for his passionate call to repentance in *An Alarm to Unconverted Sinners,* recently published under the new title *A Sure Guide to Heaven.*

Uncle to Joseph Alleine, **Richard Alleine** (1610/11–1681) began his career as an Anglican priest, but became a Puritan and subscribed to the Solemn League and Covenant in 1643, which aligned him with the parliamentary cause in the English Civil War and showed that his sympathies were with the Westminster Assembly of Divines. After the restoration, Richard was ejected from his pulpit in 1662 along with 2,000 other Puritan preachers when Charles II issued the Act of Uniformity. Richard preached in private homes and faced persecution until he died.

Known for his gentle nature and earnest piety, Puritan theologian **Isaac Ambrose** (1604–1664) was twice imprisoned and later ejected in 1662 from his Anglican pastorate for holding Puritan views. Ambrose wrote a lengthy devotional book called *Looking Unto Jesus*, which was said to have been as popular in its day as Bunyan's *Pilgrim's Progress.*

William Ames (1576–1633) was known throughout England and the Netherlands as a theologian and debater, and was noted in particular for his thoughts in the debates between Calvinists and Arminians at the Synod of Dort in 1618–1619. His thoughts became especially influential in New England through his book *The Marrow of Theology*, which was used as a textbook in colonial America for a hundred years.

Richard Baxter (1615–1691) was a Puritan church leader, poet, hymn writer, and theologian. He was notable for his tireless catechizing and visitation ministry as a curate at Kidderminster. He served prison time as a powerful preacher and an influential leader in the Nonconformist movement, once for leading an unauthorized small group. He was ejected from his pulpit in 1662, as many Puritan ministers were. His *Reformed Pastor* is one of the most-read Puritan books to this day, and his massive book on heaven, *The Saints' Everlasting Rest*, has long been celebrated as a devotional classic.

Oxford-educated **Lewis Bayly** (1575–1631) was vicar of Evesham, Worcestershire; rector of St. Matthew's Church in London; and ultimately a bishop in the Church of England. During the reigns of James I and Charles I he was persecuted—and once even imprisoned for months—because of his Puritan views. Bayly is best known for writing the classic *The Practice of Piety*, a book which was influential in John Bunyan's spiritual awakening.

Anne Bradstreet (1612–1672) was the first poet to have her works published in the British North American colonies. She came to America in 1630 from England with her Puritan husband and father. Her first poems were published in England without her knowledge and became very popular.

William Bridge (1600–1670) was a leading independent pastor, lecturer, and theologian. Because of his prominence in the Nonconformist movement and disagreement with Church of England authorities, he was forced to minister for a time in Holland, before returning to England and becoming a member of the Westminster Assembly of Divines in 1642. Along with two thousand other Puritan pastors, Bridge was ejected from his pulpit in 1662 when Charles II issued the Act of Uniformity.

Born to a wealthy family, **Thomas Brooks** (1608–1680) served a number of years at sea, probably as a chaplain. He was a pastor at Thomas Apostle's Church in London and preached to the House of Commons. Charles Spurgeon said that "Brooks scatters stars with both hands, with an eagle eye of faith as well as the eagle eye of imagination" (Preface to *Smooth Stones Taken from Ancient Brooks* [Edinburgh Carlisle, PA: Banner of Truth Trust, 2011]).

One of the most influential and best-remembered Puritan preachers, **John Bunyan** (1628–1688) spent twelve years in prison for refusing to cease his Nonconformist brand of preaching. Today he is best known for writing the Christian allegory *Pilgrim's Progress,* one of the most published books in the English language.

Anthony Burgess (1600–1663) was a member of the Westminster Assembly, a council of theologians and politicians who met from 1643 to 1653 and produced the widely used and respected Westminster Confession of Faith. A well-known Puritan, this prolific preacher and writer enthusiastically promoted Reformation ideals. A massive work Burgess wrote on assurance of salvation, which was originally published in 1652, was abridged and re-published under the title *Faith Seeking Assurance* in 2015.

Jeremiah Burroughs (1599–1646) graduated with a master's degree from Emmanuel College, Cambridge, in 1624 and later became a member of the Westminster Assembly of Divines. In 1644 he signed *An Apologetical Narration*, a manifesto supporting congregationalism and independent churches. He was a strong promoter of Christian unity; the motto on his study door (in Latin and Greek) read, "Difference of belief and unity of believers are not inconsistent." He died in 1646 after a fall from his horse. Burroughs was a prolific author, many of whose works have been reprinted in modern editions, including the devotional classics *The Rare Jewel of Christian Contentment* and *A Treatise of Earthly-Mindedness*.

Stephen Charnock (1628–1680) was converted to the faith while studying at Emmanuel College, Cambridge. He later went on to serve as a Presbyterian minister and a chaplain to Henry Cromwell, governor of Ireland. He is chiefly known for his massive volume, *The Existence and Attributes of God*, one of the greatest books on the topic ever written.

David Clarkson (1622–1686) was one of the 2,000 Puritan ministers ejected from his position in the Church of England by the 1662 Act of Uniformity. He later pastored two independent congregations. Richard Baxter commended his "solid judgment ... great ministerial abilities, and godly upright life" (*Reliquiæ Baxterianæ: Or, Mr. Richard Baxter's Narrative of the Most Memorable Passages of His Life and Times* [London: T. Parkhurst, J. Robinson, J. Lawrence, and J. Dunton, 1696]).

Puritan preacher **Arthur Dent** (died 1607) was best known for writing *The Plain Man's Pathway to Heaven,* an influential book which John Bunyan reportedly read during the spiritual struggle that led up to his conversion. Dent was a powerful preacher, and he remained rector at South Shoesbury for twenty-seven years. But he ran into trouble with Church of England authorities for refusing to sign a statement declaring that nothing in the Book of Common Prayer contradicted Scripture.

Orphaned at an early age, **Philip Doddridge** (1709–1751) declined offers to study for the Anglican priesthood and instead attended the dissenting academy at Kibworth in Leicestershire, England. He served as a preacher in the independent tradition, and he became a prolific author and hymnwriter. During several decades of pastoral ministry he took a special interest in discipling young men for church leadership and began writing books on theology and Christian living while he was in his late thirties.

Preacher and author **William Gurnall** (1616–1679) served as curate and then rector of the church at Lavenham, Suffolk, from the age of 28 until his death at age 63. During this tumultuous time, he chose to sign a declaration required by the Act of Uniformity in 1662, thus remaining in his pastorate but perhaps damaging his standing among fellow Puritans. His book *The Christian in Complete Armour* is a

classic work on spiritual warfare based on Ephesians 6:10–
20. C. H. Spurgeon spoke highly of it indeed: "Gurnall's
work is peerless and priceless; every line is full of wisdom."

William Guthrie (1620–1665) was a pastor in the Scottish
Covenanter movement, which played a key role in the
history of Scotland—as well as in Ireland, England, and
eventually the American colonies. The eldest of five sons,
he gave away his inheritance to enter pastoral ministry
unencumbered. He is known for writing *The Christian's
Great Interest*, a classic on the assurance of faith.

Robert Hawker (1753–1827) originally trained as a sur-
geon but later served as vicar in the Church of England
near Plymouth, where he is buried. Popular throughout
England for his passionate, Christ-centered preaching,
he was best known for his "Poor Man's" devotionals and
commentaries—written in a style that would be accessible
to even the poorest members of his congregation. He had
a heart for the poor, and he delighted in visiting the homes
in his parish. Charles Spurgeon said of him, "If you want
something full of marrow and fatness, cheering to your
own hearts by way of comment, and likely to help you in
giving to your hearers rich expositions, buy Dr. Hawker's
Poor Man's Commentary. ... He sees Jesus, and that is a
sacred gift which is most precious" (*Lectures to My Students:
Commenting and Commentaries; Lectures Addressed to the
Students of the Pastors' College, Metropolitan Tabernacle*, vol. 4
[New York: Sheldon & Company, 1876], 29).

Though born in Wales, Nonconformist Puritan pastor
Matthew Henry (1662–1714) spent most of his life and

ministry in England. Even today he is best known for his masterwork six-volume *Exposition of the Old and New Testaments with Practical Observations*—a verse-by-verse commentary on the Bible.

George Herbert (1593–1633) was a Welsh-born poet, speaker, and Church of England minister. He was especially known for his lyrical poetry. As a pastor, he cared deeply for his parishioners and the underprivileged. He died young at age 39. C. S. Lewis found Herbert to "excel all the authors I had ever read in conveying the very quality of life as we actually live it from moment to moment" (*Surprised by Joy: The Shape of My Early Life* [San Francisco: HarperOne, 2017], 261).

The son of a pastor, **Ezekiel Hopkins** (1633–1689) was known for his eloquent preaching, impassioned writing, and concern for the lost. He served as Bishop of Derry in the Church of Ireland from 1681 until his death.

John Howe (1630–1705) was a Puritan theologian and pastor widely known for his ability to build bridges and maintain relationships in a time of theological uncertainty. While never abandoning his Puritan roots, he was always prepared to serve believers of other schools as well.

Politically active and influential, **John Owen** (1616–1683) produced a large library of theological thought, much of which is still in print today. He is often called "the Prince of the Puritans," and some of his most influential works include *The Glory of Christ, Communion with God,* and *The Mortification of Sin.*

English Puritan pastor and scholar **Robert Parker** (1564–1614) was once reprimanded for not wearing the proper scholastic gown, and he found himself at odds with the established church after publishing a criticism of how the sign of the cross was used during religious ceremonies. Pursued by church authorities, he escaped to exile in the Netherlands, where he wrote and ministered until his death.

Edward Reynolds (1599–1676) served as Bishop of Norwich in the Church of England.ʳ He was moderate on the subject of church polity though he supported the Presbyterian movement. He was a member of the Westminster Assembly of Divines and was quite active on various committees. He also held a number of church positions and worked to reconcile with dissenters.

John Robinson (1575–1625) was pastor to the pilgrims before they left for America. As an early leader of the Separatist movement there, he helped shepherd those who would eventually leave for the New World. He died, however, before he could join the group in Massachusetts.

Richard Sibbes (1577–1635) was known as a mainline Puritan, since he remained within the Church of England his entire life and kept to the Book of Common Prayer. He was known as "the heavenly doctor" because of his godliness and his focus on the next life with Jesus. His work was influential in his own times and beyond, reaching to the American colonies and to great leaders in later generations such as John Wesley and Charles Spurgeon.

As a Nonconformist pastor, **Nathanael Vincent** (1639–1697) was frequently arrested and imprisoned for his faithful but independent views. Even so, the courageous pastor continued to preach and write throughout his career until his death at age 59.

Evangelist **George Whitefield** (1714–1770) was instrumental in spreading the Great Awakening in Britain as well as in the British North American colonies. One of the founders of Methodism, he was perhaps the best-known preacher of the eighteenth century.

Octavius Winslow (1808–1878) was born a century after the time of the Puritans, though he was known as the "Pilgrim's Companion" for his earnest preaching and devotional writing. A contemporary of Charles Spurgeon and J. C. Ryle, he served churches in America and England.

Considered a "Dutch Puritan," influential theologian **Herman Witsius** (1636–1708) is known for his landmark writings on covenant theology. He was a professor of divinity at several Dutch universities and was fluent in Latin, Greek, and Hebrew at age fifteen.

Index of Authors

Sources Quoted

Modern editions are listed where possible. It is difficult to establish with certainty the original publication date of some of these works; educated guesses sometimes are provided.

Joseph Alleine (1634–1668)

The Saint's Pocket Book (London: William Tegg, 1866). Original publication, 1666?

A Sure Guide to Heaven (Carlisle, PA: Banner of Truth, 1960). Original publication, 1671?

A Soliloquy for an Unregenerate Sinner (London: Thomas Parkhurst, 1691).

Richard Alleine (1610/11–1681)

Heaven Opened: A Brief and Plain Discovery of the Riches of God's Covenant of Grace (New York: American Tract Society, 1853). Original publication, 1665?

Isaac Ambrose (1604–1664)

The Works of Isaac Ambrose (London: Thomas Allen, 1799).

WILLIAM AMES (1576–1633)

The Saint's Security Against Seducing Spirits (London: M. Simmons, 1652).

RICHARD BAXTER (1615–1691)

The Practical Works of the Late Reverend and Pious Richard Baxter (London: Thomas Parkhurst, 1707).

The Saint's Everlasting Rest: Or, A Treatise of the Blessed State of the Saints in Their Enjoyment of God in Glory; extracted from the works of Mr. Richard Baxter, by John Wesley, M.A., late fellow of Lincoln College, Oxford (Philadelphia: printed by Prichard & Hall, in Market Street, and sold by John Dickins, in Fourth Street, no. 43 near Race Street, 1790).

LEWIS BAYLY (1575–1631)

The Practice of Piety: A Puritan Devotional Manual (Grand Rapids: Soli Deo Gloria Publications, 2019).

ANNE BRADSTREET (1612–1672)

The Works of Anne Bradstreet in Prose and Verse, ed. John Harvard Ellis (Charlestown: Abram E. Cutter, 1867).

WILLIAM BRIDGE (1600–1670)

The Works of the Rev. William Bridge, M.A., 3 vols. (London: Thomas Tegg, 1845).

Thomas Brooks (1608–1680)

The Mute Christian under the Smarting Rod; with Sovereign Antidotes for Every Case, 48th ed. (London: W. Nicholson, 1806).

John Bunyan (1628–1688)

Grace Abounding to the Chief of Sinners (Carlisle, PA: Banner of Truth, 2018). Original publication, 1666?

"A prayer 1681, at the church in Hitchin, founded by Bunyan; probably written by him," in *Israel's Hope Encouraged*; no publication information available.

Anthony Burgess (1600–1663)

The True Doctrine of Justification: Asserted, and Vindicated, from the Errors of Papists, Arminians, Socinians, and More Especially Antinomians (London: Robert White, 1648).

Jeremiah Burroughs (1599–1646)

The Saint's Treasury (London: John Wright, 1654).

The Saints' Happiness, Together with the Several Steps Leading Thereunto (Edinburgh: James Nichol, 1867), originally published 1659 or 1660.

Irenicum, *to the Lovers of Truth and Peace* (London: Robert Dawlman, 1653).

Stephen Charnock (1628–1680)

Two Discourses: The First, Of Man's Enmity to God; The Second, Of the Salvation of Sinners (London: Thomas Cockerill, at the Three Legs and Bible in the Poultrey, over-against Grocers-Hall, 1699).

David Clarkson (1622–1686)

The Works of David Clarkson, B.D. (Edinburgh: John Greig and Son, Old Physic Gardens, n.d.).

Arthur Dent (died 1607)

The Plain Man's Pathway to Heaven; Wherein Every Man May Clearly See Whether He Shall Be Saved or Damned, 50th ed. (Belfast: North of Ireland Book & Tract Depository, 1859), originally published 1601.

Philip Doddridge (1709–1751)

The Works of Rev. P. Doddridge, D.D. in Ten Volumes (Leeds: Edward Raines, 1802).

The Rise and Progress of Religion in the Soul: Illustrated in a Course of Serious and Practical Addresses, Suited to Persons of Every Character and Circumstance: Wtih a Devout Meditation or Prayer Added to Each Chapter, 8th ed. (London: Hitch and Hawes, 1761).

William Gurnall (1616–1679)

The Christian in Complete Armour; A Treatise of the Saints' War against the Devil: Wherein a Discovery Is Made of

That Grand Enemy of God and His People, in His Policies, Power, Seat of His Empire, Wickedness, and Chief Design He Hath against the Saints. A Magazine Opened from whence the Christian Is Furnished with Spiritual Arms for the Battle, Helped on with His Armour, and Taught the Use of His Weapon: Together with the Happy Issue of the Whole War (London: Blackie and Son, Paternoster Row, 1845), originally published in three volumes from 1655 to 1662.

WILLIAM GUTHRIE (1620–1665)

The Christian's Great Interest (Glasgow: William Collins, 1828). Original publication, 1668?

ROBERT HAWKER (1753–1827)

Poor Man's Morning and Evening Portions (London, 1829).

MATTHEW HENRY (1662–1714)

A Method for Prayer: With Scripture Expressions, Proper to Be Used under Each Head; With Directions for Daily Communion with God, Showing How to Begin, How to Spend, and How to Close Every Day with God (Glasgow: D. Mackenzie, 1834).

GEORGE HERBERT (1593–1633)

A Preist to the Temple, Or The Countrey Parson His Character, and Rule of Holy Life (London: T. Maxey for T. Garthwait, 1652).

Life of the Rev. George Herbert (London: Religious Tract Society, n.d.).

Ezekiel Hopkins (1633–1689)

The Works of Ezekiel Hopkins, D.D, Successively Bishop of Raphe and Derry (London, 1809).

John Howe (1630–1705)

The Works of John Howe, M.A. (London: Religious Tract Society, 1862).

John Owen (1616–1683)

The Glory of Christ (Fearn, Ross-shire, Scotland: Christian Focus Publications, 2004).

Robert Parker (1564–1614)

The Devout Soul's Daily Exercise in Prayers, Contemplations, and Praises (London, 1740).

Edward Reynolds (1599–1676)

The Whole Works of the Right Rev. Edward Reynolds, D.D. (London, 1826).

John Robinson (1575–1625)

The Works of John Robinson: Pastor of the Pilgrim Fathers (London: John Snow, 1851).

Richard Sibbes (1577–1635)

The Bruised Reed (Edinburgh: Banner of Truth Trust, 1998).

Nathanael Vincent (1639–1697)

The Spirit of Prayer, Or, A Discourse Wherein the Nature of Prayer Is Opened, the Kindes of Prayer Are Handled, and the Right Manner of Praying Discovered: Several Cases about this Duty Are Resolved (London: Tho. Parkhurst, 1677).

George Whitefield (1714–1770)

A Continuation of the Reverend Mr. Whitefield's Journal, from a Few Days After His Arrival at Savannah, June the Fourth, to His Leaving Stanford, the Last Town in New-England, October 29. 1740 (Philadelphia: Printed and Sold by B. Franklin, 1741).

Octavius Winslow (1808–1878)

"Trial, a Help Heavenward." No bibliographical information available; provenance uncertain.

Herman Witsius (1636–1708)

The Oeconomy of the Covenants between God and Man: Comprehending a Complete Body of Divinity (London: Edward Dilly, 1762).